C0-ARP-727

*A Still Small Voice*

# A Still Small Voice

by

## E. F. ENGELBERT

*Pastor Emeritus*

*Martini Lutheran Church*

*Baltimore, Md.*

WILLIAM B. EERDMANS PUBLISHING COMPANY

GRAND RAPIDS, MICHIGAN

© *Copyright 1964 by Wm. B. Eerdmans Publishing Company.*
*All rights reserved. Printed in the United States of America.*
*Library of Congress catalog card number, 64-8906.*

*With love and appreciation*
*I dedicate this book to my wife,*
*Clara Engelbert,*
*to whom I freguently read a sermon before it was preached.*
*Always she was my fairest as well as my severest critic.*

# Foreword

Another volume of sermons! But not *just* another. There is something different about these sermons. For one thing, they are unusually short. No "elongated vacuity" here, no pompous rhetoric or gaudy verbiage, but compact, well-built sermons, characterized by unity of thought and purpose.

The language, simple and chaste, flows along in smooth and pleasant cadences — easy to read, easy to listen to.

Marked by a mature and unobtrusive Biblical scholarship untarnished by ancient doubts and modern liberalism, these sermons preach the good old Gospel of Christ in messages that are clear, positive, and authoritative, firmly grounded in the inspired Word. And yet they contain things hitherto undiscovered by many of us, especially in the areas of historical reference and the application of old truths to new situations.

Page after page in this volume bears witness to the fact that these sermons were not written for the printing press but for the pulpit, and that the man who wrote them is not a mere pulpiteer but an experienced and dedicated shepherd of souls. He never preaches divine truth in a vacuum or in the cold abstractions of a theological theorist, but always in direct relation to the problems of his people and with a warm pastoral affection born out of the sorrows and joys of a long and fruitful ministry.

At a class reunion several years ago, the author described his father's reactions to two sermons which he heard him preach in his early ministry. In the first instance, his father proudly commended him for his forthright Christ-centered preaching. In the second instance, he severely censured him for having buried Christ under a conglomeration of pious platitudes and sterile moralizing. Apparently neither the commendation nor the censure was wasted, for the sermons in this volume constitute a clear and uncompromising testimony to our blessed Saviour.

It is a pleasure for us, therefore, to commend these sermons to the attention of our brethren and to wish them Godspeed on their far-flung mission.

E. J. FRIEDRICH

# Preface

The sermons herein published were for the most part preached in Martini Lutheran Church of Baltimore during the thirty-nine years of the author's pastorate in that congregation. There was no thought of publication when they were written. It was only at the close of a ministry of almost half a century, and with the urging of brother ministers, that they were prepared for print. It was done then only in the hope that they may be of some help to busy pastors in the preparation of their own presentation of the ever glorious message of salvation in Jesus Christ, our blessed Saviour. A better reward would not be possible.

E. F. ENGELBERT

# Contents

## CONTENTS

# 1

## *John the Baptist*

The Greatest in the Old Testament—the Least in the New Testament

### (Advent)
### John 1:23

*He said, I am the voice of one crying in the wilderness, Make straight the way of the Lord, as said the prophet Esaias.*

John the Baptist is the one heroic, dominating figure of Advent, until Christ Himself appears upon the scene. John carried his credentials with him in the book of Isaiah, who centuries before had introduced him to the faithful and had identified him as "the voice of him that cryeth in the wilderness, Prepare ye the way of the LORD, make straight in the desert a highway for our God."

Way-preparing was not a new thing for the people of John's day. It was a profession. The Romans had a name for men engaged in way-preparing. They called them *"stratores."* When Eastern monarchs took a journey through desert or mountain country, they sent men before them to prepare the way.

Deodorus in his account of the march of Semiramis into Media and Persia gives us a description of the preparations of a way for a royal expedition. In her march Semiramis came to the Zarcean mountain, a terrain full of craggy precipices

and deep ravines, which could not be passed without extended
and wearisome detours. At tremendous expense she ordered
the precipices to be graded down and the ravines to be filled
up, thus smoothing and easing the way. To this day it is
called the Road of Semiramis.

When the time came for the King of Israel to make His
appearance, John was sent to prepare His way, as Isaiah foretold: "Every valley shall be exalted, and every mountain and
hill shall be made low; and the crooked shall be made straight,
and the rough places plain."

John's work was of a dual nature. He was the way-preparer
of the Lord, and he was His herald, sent to announce His
coming. "Repent ye: for the kingdom of heaven is at hand."
Heralds were commissioned to proclaim in streets, fields, and
open air what was committed to them by regal or public
authority. Thus John, the herald, came to proclaim tidings of
great and solemn importance to men, to announce that the
King of kings was near to establish His kingdom, of which
Daniel had so long ago said, "His dominion is an everlasting
dominion, which shall not pass away, and his kingdom that
which shall not be destroyed."

John was a voice in the wilderness, in a wilderness typical
of the Jewish church, destitute of truly religious cultivation
and of the spirit and practice of faith. And that is all John
claimed for himself; that is all he desired to be, a voice, proclaiming the coming of the Lord.

Humanly speaking, John could have been much more than
a mere voice. John was a rugged, striking character who would
have stood forth among men in any age and under all circumstances. Jesus placed him on a high pedestal indeed, when He
styled him the greatest man ever born of woman up to that
time. Pharaoh, Nebuchadnezzar, Alexander, Plato, Aristotle,
Moses, Daniel, and David all are great in our eyes even to
this late date; John, however, Jesus said, was greater than
these, greater than all others. Luke tells us that John performed in the "spirit and power of Elias." Self-effacing,
rugged, dynamic, like Elias, he worked with the same single-
ness of purpose, to the one end of turning men to Christ
through repentance and faith. He cared nothing for material

ease and comfort. He wore a garment of camel's hair and ate locusts and wild honey.

Some years ago, in the famous sunken garden of Bermuda, I saw a locust tree, transplanted from Palestine. Had I come two weeks later, the gardener informed me, I might have tasted of its cone-shaped fruit, and he assured me that dipped in honey it is delicious. But who would want it for a steady diet? However, it appeased John's hunger, and he asked for no more.

John was great because he was the last of the prophets, and the only one who could point the finger of identification at Jesus and say, "This is He!" What all other prophets saw only in prophetic vision, he saw with his own eyes. He was great in his courage and fearlessness. He knew what was in store for him if he should go to Herod and rebuke him for his adultery. In that day kings were kings, to whom human life was cheap, and to oppose them meant death. But John had a duty to perform, and there could be no debating with himself. John was great in his eloquence and in his power of attraction. To go out there to Bethabara to hear him preach meant for people to close shop and factory, to forego profits and conveniences, to face hunger and hardship; but drawn by his dynamic, personal powers, they went — all Jerusalem and the regions round about. There had never been anything like it.

Above all, John was great in his complete self-effacement. One day a group of priests and Levites came to John. They had been sent, which can only mean that they were delegated by the Sanhedrin, to question John. Luke tells us, "The people were in expectation." From Daniel's prophecy of the "seventy weeks" their learned men had rightly concluded that the time was at hand for Messiah to make His appearance. This brought about a great revival of hope in Israel. It accounts also for the great crowds which again flocked to Jerusalem for the festivals. First, however, according to prophecy, Elias was to come. This Elias, as Jesus so plainly stated, was John the Baptist. The rabbis had interpreted this prophecy to mean that the old Elijah would return shortly before the appearance of the Messiah. When John told them that he was not that Elijah, they asked, "Art thou that prophet?" Moses had foretold that God would raise up a prophet. Here again they had misinterpreted. Moses referred to the Messiah Himself. They expected the return of Jeremiah, who they said would restore to them the ark of the covenant, which they thought he had hidden to save it from capture by the Babylonians. When John again denied being that prophet, they no longer hesitated but asked, "Art thou the Christ?"

No man ever faced a greater temptation than John did when that delegation came to him. There had been many false prophets and false Christs, all of whom had come to a sorry end because they were not accepted. And here John was offered, on a silver platter, as it were, the highest honor and dignity men could bestow. The excitement of the people and the attitude of the Sanhedrin would have assured his ascendancy had he been willing to go hand in hand with the blind leaders of the blind. Jesus said, John was the greatest of all. What would have been almost an irresistible temptation to a weaker man did not tempt him at all. Without a moment's hesitancy he asked, as it were, "Why ask who I am? I am nothing. I am merely a voice; I am merely preparing the way of another."

As soon as a man, be he saint or sinner, comes into the presence of Christ, his virtues, achievements, appearances of greatness, and powers of personality are completely overshadowed. It was so with John. Like a mighty army, all Jerusalem, Judea, and the regions round about had followed him. But soon there was only a corporal's guard left with him. All were instead following Jesus, to hear Him. Had Herod imprisoned John a year earlier, the people, no doubt, would have stormed the palace to release him. Now he languished in loneliness. His disciples could not understand it, but he did. "He must increase, and I must decrease" — to him it was as simple as that.

Had John succumbed to the temptation to acclaim himself the Messiah, we would know as little of him as we know of other false prophets and false Christs who preceded him. But because he steadfastly insisted that he was only a voice proclaiming that for which he had been sent, he is still heard. Again, in this Advent season, we hear the old familiar cry,

"Repent ye: for the kingdom of heaven is at hand."

God designed that the kingdom of grace here below should resemble the kingdom of glory above. "Behold thy king cometh." He rules over His church, and His church is a kingdom, because it has laws, subjects, and a sovereign. Its law is the new commandment of love; its subjects are all who believe in Christ; its Sovereign is He through whom all things were made, Christ, the eternal Son of God. At His birth the song of the angels was a song of "Glory." At the beginning of His Passion, as He entered Jerusalem to die, the people sang, "Hosanna," which means "Lord, save us." At Easter, the day of resurrection, the song of the Church is "Halleluiah," which means "Give praise to the Lord." We can join in the Halleluiah chorus only if we first join in the Hosanna, and we can do that only if we heed the Advent cry of the Baptist, "Repent!"

On that first Advent the people sang "Hosanna" — "Save us." And as they sang, He had His eyes steadfastly set on the cross. Inexorably the cross beckoned because there was no other way to save us, to save us from our sins. "By his stripes we are healed." The Advent multitude, as well as His disciples, awaited glory, the glory of a worldly kingdom. He, too, awaited glory — but a glory that could come only through the shame of the cross.

As you prepare for the celebration of Christmas, do not let the material side of our Christmas crowd out the true meaning of Christmas. Think of your sins, which necessitated His earthly life and dominated it from the humble manger all the way to the shameful cross. "Repent," and pray the Holy Spirit to help you sing, "Hosanna," "Lord, save me." Only thus can you at Christmas and Easter sing, "Glory!" and "Halleluiah!" *Amen.*

# 2

## *Christ, Expected by All Nations*

### (Advent)
### Haggai 2:6-7

*For thus saith the* LORD *of hosts, Yet once, it is a little while, and I will shake the heavens, and the earth, and the sea, and the dry land; And I will shake all nations, and the desire of all nations shall come: and I will fill this house with glory, saith the* LORD *of hosts.*

The Advent Season always comes as a mandate to occupy ourselves with Messianic prophecies, of which there are many. The ancient rabbis were wont to say, "The prophets spake not but of the Messiah." All commentators are agreed that Haggai in this text gives voice to a Messianic prophecy, but there is much disagreement when the words "and the desire of all nations shall come" are under consideration.

The Vulgate, the Authorized Version, and Luther's Translation, all identify the "desire of all nations" with the Messiah Himself. Others hold that these words refer to the costly things which the different nations should bring into the Temple.

We are so accustomed to the terms "Messiah of Israel," "King of Israel," "Promised One of Israel," "Salvation of

Israel," that it sounds strange to hear Him spoken of as "the desire of all nations." Nevertheless, that is what God intended Him to be. It would be a gross exaggeration to say all nations were looking for a Saviour from sin, and it would be a gross understatement to say only Israel expected a Messiah. The tradition at least that a Messiah should come was universal.

We can readily understand how the promise of God, given to Adam and Eve after the fall into sin, was kept alive in the antediluvian world. According to Genesis 5, Adam still lived when Methuselah, the grandfather of Noah, was born. These three generations overlapped the entire age from the creation to the flood. During these long years the coming of the Saviour was not only spoken of by Adam, Methuselah, and Noah, but also by their pious sons and daughters. When Noah, while he built the ark, preached repentance and faith, what else could he have preached but the coming of the Lord?

Abraham, in Ur of the Chaldees, was a believer when God called him out of his country. Moreover, God gave him the promise that the Messiah should come from his seed, and that all nations should be blessed in Him. But Abraham was not the only believer. Certainly the three sons of Noah, Shem, Ham, and Japheth, spoke of the Messiah wherever and whenever opportunity offered itself. And Shem was a contemporary of Abraham. Not only was he still living in Abraham's day, but he outlived him by 45 years. The ancient rabbis insisted that Shem was Melchizedek, priest and king in Salem, which was later called Jerusalem. In this Luther concurred. They knew each other, perhaps for many years. At any rate Melchizedek feasted and blessed Abraham when the latter returned from the battle against the four kings. From Noah to Abraham covers the span of the four hundred years following the flood. Another contemporary of Abraham was Hammurabi, king of Babylon. The modern world rediscovered Hammurabi in the year 1902, when archeological excavations brought to light his code of laws and many other writings. Hammurabi is identified with the Amraphel of the Bible, one of the kings who fought against Abraham. It would be farfetched to assume that a man of his intelligence and literary ability knew nothing of the religion of such contemporaries as Abraham and Melchizedek.

We can safely say that the world in Abraham's day had knowledge of the coming of a Messiah. And we can say that with even greater safety of the centuries following his death. Abraham's two sons, Isaac and Ishmael, came to the parting of their ways, but they were still one Church and shared the same faith in a coming Saviour. God gave Isaac the blessing that the Messiah should come from his seed; and he blessed Ishmael also, promising to make of him twelve nations. How Isaac kept the promise alive in his part of the world we know; how it was kept alive in the Eastern countries after Ishmael's death is conjecture. To this day, however, visitors to Mecca are shown the graves of Hagar and Ishmael, and the Moslems still claim that Ishmael and not Isaac was the son of promise. Four hundred years after Abraham the true God and the promise He gave were still known in Mesopotamia, for when Balak sent for Balaam to curse Israel, he blessed instead, and prophesied of the Star that should come out of Jacob and of the Sceptre that should rise out of Israel.

In Solomon's day the Queen of Sheba came to Jerusalem, and how much of the Messianic hope she carried back with her, and how widely she spread knowledge of it, is evidenced by the fact that to this day the emperor of Ethiopia calls himself, "The Lion of the House of Judah." Moreover, we read that all the kings of the earth came to Solomon to learn of his wisdom, and while there they must have learned of his religion and of Israel's hope.

Time does not permit us to touch upon all the evidences that corroborate the fact that He came as the desire of all nations. Esau, Jacob's brother, married three Canaanitish women, from which sprang the kingdoms of the Hittite Empire, outranked in size and wealth only by the Assyro-Babylonian and Egyptian Empires. Luther says that Esau unquestionably converted many to the faith of Isaac. Among the Edomites, direct descendants of Esau, the rite of circumcision was maintained. It would be strange, indeed, if this was done without some knowledge of the true God and of the promise He gave. Job lived in Idumea, and scholars generally are in agreement that his language and style prove him an Idumean by birth, and not a Jew; and it was Job who wrote the words, "I know that my redeemer liveth."

Daniel in Babylon and Jonah in Nineveh were witnesses of the coming One. On the morning after Daniel's release from the lion's den, King Darius wrote unto all people, nations, and languages that dwell on the earth, decreeing that only the God of Daniel should be worshipped. Certainly such a decree presupposed some knowledge of Daniel's faith and of Israel's hope.

We might here quote the words ascribed to Socrates, Plato, Zoroaster, and even Confucius, indicating that they, too, knew of the promise of a coming Messiah.

Three hundred years before the fulfillment, the Hebrew Old Testament was translated into Greek, the universal language, enabling men everywhere to read the prophecies for themselves. We also know that shortly before Christ appeared, the festivals in Jerusalem were attended by mighty throngs, coming "out of every nation under heaven." As they returned to their own countries, the knowledge of the promise went with them, and was proclaimed.

When Cortez came to Mexico he was received with open arms by the natives because there existed a tradition that one day God would come to them. Even that misplaced trust might be traceable to the universal tradition that a Messiah should come.

Yes, among the many illustrious titles which, like precious gems, form a crown for our Lord to wear in glory, not the least is this, "the desire of all nations."

When the Wise Men saw the star, they were convinced that a great and wonderful thing had come to pass. Quickly came the logical deduction that the star proclaimed the birth of the Messiah; for though they lived at a great distance from Israel, they knew that the Messiah should come. It required only comforting assurance from God Himself to send them forth on their long trek.

For the Christian it is a thrilling experience to journey back and forth in the Word of God during the Advent weeks. He can start in the dimness of the past, when a prophecy was spoken, and then move forward with the unfolding centuries until he comes to the fulfillment. Or, he can start with the fulfillment and go back to the day when the prophecy was uttered, and see how marvelously God controlled all things to the end that the prophecy was fulfilled.

Scripture foretold that He should come from Abraham's seed, from David's royal line; it foretold that He should be born of a virgin, in Bethlehem, that God should call Him out of Egypt, and that He should be called a Nazarene. All these, and all other prophecies, were fulfilled in Him, and in Him alone. He is the Christ, the Desire of all nations.

Thank God that we have a sure prophetic word. We say of a man that he gambled on his future, that he took a chance, that he staked everything on his judgment concerning the character of someone. Well, we do stake everything, even our eternal salvation, on our judgment of Christ. However, we do not gamble. We are sure. Let others frantically seek another saviour; let them torture themselves in their effort to atone for their sins; let them face death in despair; let them mourn in their hopelessness when their dear ones die; we are calm, happy, and filled with peace because we know, because we are sure.

In Him we have forgiveness through His blood. God laid our sins upon Him, and we gratefully leave them there. We do not take them back because we know that He has atoned for them, has reconciled us unto God, and has made us heirs of salvation. We know this from the Word of God, which cannot be broken. Every word of prophecy was fulfilled by Him: He will also fulfill His sacred promise given to us, that He will in the end receive us into eternal life. *Amen.*

# 3

## The Angel's "Unto You" Means You

### (Christmas Eve)
### Luke 2:11

*For unto you is born this day in the city of David a Saviour, which is Christ the Lord.*

Here in our city, night after night, we see the sky aglow over the great Bethlehem Steel Works. On this night, however, the sky over the Bethlehem Steel Works is dark, because 1900 years ago, in this holy night, the sky was aglow over the little town of Bethlehem, in distant Judea.

Not far from here, in Bethlehem of Pennsylvania, men are gazing at a huge star, composed of electric lights, erected on one of the high hills, overlooking the city. And the entire Bethlehem is illumined, as perhaps no other city in America. Myriads of lights reflect the joy of the citizens in the consciousness that their city is named after the little town of Bethlehem, in faraway Judea.

It is the birthday of our Lord, and no other event could turn out the lights of industry and turn on the lights of festivity in all the lands where eyes are turned toward Bethlehem of Judea, to behold again the first wondrous Christmas service.

Shepherds were watching their sheep. These were neither ordinary shepherds, nor ordinary sheep. Here in Bethlehem's fields were kept the sheep which were destined to be sacrificed in the temple. It was most appropriate that these shepherds should first receive the announcement of the birth of the Lamb of God, to be slain for the sins of the world. They who watched over sacrificial sheep were now to see the sacrificial Lamb whom their sheep had merely foreshadowed.

Once before the song of heaven rang out over all the earth; namely when, at the creation, "the morning stars sang together, and all the sons of God shouted for joy." Now, at the beginning of man's recreation the sons of God came again with a song, whose echo fills the sky in this holy night. And the preacher, when he came from the very presence of God, preached a sermon of such incomprehensible sublimity, that he himself could not fully understand it. The choir translated the preacher's message into praise. He spoke of a lowly manger, they sang "Glory!"

The ground theme of the service was "unto you." "I bring you good tidings." That was the first "unto you." Now came the second, "unto you is born a Saviour." And then followed the third, "And this shall be a sign unto you."

The purpose of this thrice-repeated "unto you," was to fill their hearts with certainty. Like a golden thread it ran through the entire sermon. I bring *you* glad tidings; unto *you* is born; a sign unto *you*. Even an angel could not overemphasize this "unto you." The humble shepherds must have wondered why the angel should bring such a message to them, who were men of low degree. Why not to the king? Why not to the high priest? Why not from the pinnacle of the temple to all the people of Jerusalem? It was to allay all such misgivings that the angel made this "unto you" so strong.

We need the same strong assurance that the angel's "unto you" embraces us also. Standing in the searching light of Christmas, we, too, are sometimes "sore afraid."

We are Adam's children. In him and with him we turned our backs on God, insulted our Creator, and became His irreconcilable enemies. Enemies do not receive gifts from enemies, except when the weaker gives to the strong, and pays tribute to escape further punishment. But here comes the angel to tell us that God has bestowed upon us, His enemies, weak and helpless over against Him and already in the grip of death, heaven's greatest gift. Why such a gift to His enemies, who did not ask for it, who did not even want it?

Like the shepherds, we need strong assurance if we are to shed our fears and believe that the "unto you" enfolds us also. Thank God, we have it. The angel said the glad tidings should be "to all people." That can only mean mankind, men anywhere, men everywhere. If we are people, we are included.

The angels did not sing to themselves. They had no part in God's great gift. They could not even understand, no matter how much "they desired to look into it." But they knew it meant the salvation of man. Horrified, they had fled from the cursed earth when Adam sinned. Now, however, the Saviour from sin was born, and joyfully they return to preach and sing, "unto you."

Let us shed our fears; let us take up this "unto you" and make it "unto us." "Unto us a child is born, unto us a son is given . . .; and his name shall be called Wonderful, Counselor, The mighty God, The everlasting Father, The Prince of Peace." Let us, as the shepherds did, join our song to theirs. They "returned, glorifying and praising God for all the things that they had heard and seen. . . ."

As we do that on earth we may hope to do it in heaven, with the angels of Isaiah's vision, who sang their *Sanctus* to Christ our Lord, "Holy, holy, holy, is the Lord of Sabaoth."

As the Holy Spirit gives us faith to believe this glorious "unto you," let us make it known to all men yet in darkness. "Which shall be known to all people." That is our part — to make it known abroad, so that ever greater and greater may be the chorus that sings, "Glory to God in the highest and on earth peace, good will toward men." *Amen.*

# 4

## *The Christmas Light in the Blackout*

### (Christmas)
### Isaiah 9:2

*The people that walked in darkness have seen a great light:
they that dwell in the land of the shadow of death, upon them
hath the light shined.*

The dictionaries of living languages experience continual growth. Wars, the discoveries of modern science, medical research, political alliances and machinations, the achievements of engineering, even children's games and toys put words, never before spoken, in the mouths of people.

Such a word is "blackout." It was born during World War II. It resulted from the attempt of cities and municipalities to cover themselves with darkness during enemy air raids. There were, however, no complete blackouts. Always there were the careless; moreover the lights of industry could not hurriedly be extinguished.

The only complete blackout in the history of mankind came as the result of sin. Then darkness truly covered the earth, and gross darkness the people. It was the only time that the prince of darkness ever succeeded to make man, God's foremost creature, to grope in absolute darkness. But even this one complete blackout was of short duration. God lit a candle. He gave the first promise of a coming Saviour, the promise of "the woman's seed," which was to "bruise the serpent's head."

The blackout that settled upon Eden endured for many long centuries. Even then our loving God took no delight in the death of the wicked. He, even then, wanted men to be saved. To help men find the way to salvation He, again and again, repeated that first promise and enlarged upon it. During the long blackout the prophecies appeared, as beacon lights do to the mariner. The nearer the time of fulfillment came the closer they were spaced, the clearer they shone forth.

The prophecies disclosed that the woman's seed should spring from the nation which God expressly created for the purpose of centering the preparations for the Saviour's coming, when He called Abraham to come out from among his people to become the progenitor of His chosen race. The Saviour was to come from the tribe of Judah; from David's royal line; born of a virgin. Bethlehem was His designated birthplace. He was to appear seventy weeks, seven times seventy years, four hundred and ninety years, after the decree was signed in Babylon, which permitted Israel to return to its homeland to build the temple in which He was personally to appear.

Then came a glorious burst of light, when the sky of the holy night was lit up by the glory of the heavenly host, as it appeared to the frightened shepherds. But this flash of light, which so startled the shepherds, did not yet completely dispel the blackout which had covered the earth. It was seen by only a few; it soon dimmed out again. It was just the dawning light which gave promise of a new day. It was the dayspring, heralding the birth of the Dayspring from on high.

The "great light" of Isaiah's vision came with the preaching of the Gospel.

It was the Gospel-light which Isaiah envisioned as the great light seen by the people who sat in darkness. In the verse immediately preceding our text the prophet speaks of Zebulun and Naphtali. These countries around the Sea of Gennesareth were the principal sufferers in the first Assyrian invasion. They were to see the great light first of all. They were also the first to enjoy the blessings of Christ's preaching; and they were the first to see His mighty miracles.

Christ is the "Light of the world." He so named Himself. And He is so revealed in the Gospel. That is what Isaiah foretold in this text; and that is what he foresaw when he wrote, "Then shall thy light break forth," and again, "Then shall thy light rise in obscurity," "the Gentiles shall come to thy light." The psalmist said, "In thy light shall we see light," and again, "O send out thy light and thy truth." All the writers of the Gospel invite us to bask in the light of the Gospel. From Matthew, who speaks of the fulfillment of Isaiah's prophecy and says the people of Zebulun and Nephtali saw the great light, to John in Revelation, who says the nations that are saved shall walk in it, there is the oft-repeated assurance that the Gospel is the light which can penetrate any blackout anywhere.

Christmas is the festival of lights. Men tell us that the festival of lights is of pagan origin. No doubt, pagan people did celebrate the return of light after the night of winter, but for us there is a far sublimer significance. We celebrate the festival of lights because it marks the birthday of the "true Light that shineth in darkness." The pagan world in all its ancient glory never knew such a festival of lights as we celebrate today. Egypt boasts of the Mosque of a Thousand Candles. We have thousands of churches which today glow in the light of a thousand candlepower.

On a day before Christmas I saw New York City in its Christmas finery. In Rockefeller Center stood a huge Christmas tree, all aglow with thousands of lights. The windows of stores and shops along Park Avenue were radiant with nativity scenes and other beaming decorations. On both sides, block after block, the street was lined with Christmas trees, all trimmed with bright lights. And far in the distance, formed by the lighted windows of a huge skyscraper there shone out above the city a great cross. Another year I saw the Mart in Chicago, the largest mercantile building in the world under a light-effect which made one entire wall appear as a gigantic canvas, depicting a Christmas scene, with a tremendous Christmas greeting. Yes, our entire country is almost transfigured by the lights of Christmas. And in a lesser degree this is true of many other countries also.

However, no matter how impressive our display of Christmas lights may be, its real significance is lost unless we see it as a reminder of the much greater and much brighter light of Isaiah's vision, the light of the Gospel. Unfortunately even in our enlightened land many still sit in darkness. Even in many Christian churches sermons are preached today without any mention of a Saviour from sin. God created man in His own image, but ever since the fall into sin men have endeavored to create God in their own image. The heathen are not alone in this that they carve and paint things in their own images, and then call them gods. In many sermons today Christ will be created in the image of man; for He will be stripped of His divinity and held up merely as an illustrious example. Let us remind ourselves again and again that the most precious word in the angel's message, the word which, in the light of the opened heavens, reflected all the grace and love of God, is the word "Saviour." "Unto you is born this day a Saviour" — that is the brightest ray in the Gospel light.

A Saviour we need. Sin, which drove man out from the presence of God and closed the door of Paradise behind him, also condemned man to eternal death. And from that verdict man could not appeal. Man was lost, eternally lost. It was only God's own incomprehensible grace which prompted Him to reconcile the world unto Himself, and to take away the sin of the world. But the grace of God, forgiveness of sin through the atoning blood of Christ, must be personally accepted, or participation in the redemption is forfeited. And it is only by faith, by faith wrought by the Gospel, that man can lay hold on the grace of God. The Gospel is not any earthly thing, but the power of God through which the Holy Spirit leads men out of darkness to the marvelous light.

This true meaning of Christmas is impressed upon you most forcibly here in your church. As you look about you, you see how all the world has contributed something to your Christmas enjoyment. Our tree comes from British Columbia; the holly in the windows from England; the ornaments on the tree from Germany; the lights from Japan; the poinsettias on the altar from Florida; one of the hymns we sang from Austria; the anthem from France. It is all for you. And then comes the far sublimer thought — and the Child in the manger is for me. He was born for me, to save me from my sins. That is what you came here to hear; that is your true Christmas joy; that is what you joyfully confess as you join the songs of praise, which you have heard and sung since the day of your childhood. It is Christmas, because your Saviour is born. That is what you would like to shout out to all the world; for He is not your Saviour only, He is the Saviour of all men.

As the sun shines on all the earth, so the light of Isaiah's vision, the light of the Gospel, shines on all men. The far-flung outposts of our occupational forces have funneled Christmas cards into our homes from all parts of the world. Last year I received cards from Persia, India, Japan, and Alaska. The Persian card depicted a Persian nativity. The Babe in the manger was a Persian baby, Joseph and Mary were Persians, and so were the shepherds. The Alaskan card showed an Eskimo baby, the Japanese card a Japanese baby, and the Indian card an Indian baby. And rightly so. He is the true brother of all races and peoples. The angel said, "I bring you good tidings of great joy which shall be to all people."

Let us not only pray that the light of the glorious Christmas Gospel may continue to shine on us, but let us cause the light to shine on those who still sit in darkness. They need it; God wills it. *Amen.*

# 5

## The Father's Will in the New Year

### (New Year's Eve)
### Matthew 21:28-31

*But what think ye? A certain man had two sons; and he came to the first, and said, Son, go work today in my vineyard. He answered and said, I will not: but afterward he repented, and went. And he came to the second, and said likewise. And he answered and said, I go, sir: and went not. Whether of them twain did the will of his father? They say unto him, The first. Jesus saith unto them, Verily I say unto you, That the publicans and the harlots go into the kingdom of God before you.*

A few in this New Year's Eve audience were born before the turn of the century. It was a strange sensation to step out of the nineteenth century into the twentieth century. Perhaps half a dozen of you are now where you were then, here in your church. It really does not seem long ago. But here we are, well in the second half of the century. And we are showing the wear and tear of our years. We, who saw the emergence of a new century, will not see it a second time. Our allotment of time has almost been spent.

The years were made hectic by terrible wars, but they were

made interesting by the discoveries of science. More changes were made in the mode of living than in any other period in history. When you today drive an automobile, or write with a fountain pen; when you ride on an airplane, or reach for a book of matches; when you take an ice cube from your refrigerator, or set a percolator on your stove; when you cool yourself with an electric fan, or warm yourself with an electric blanket, you are doing what no one did at the turn of the century. We type a letter and send it air mail; we pick up a telephone on the east coast and dial someone on the west coast; we send rockets into outer space and speak of a visit to the moon.

How much did we contribute to the sensational developments of our time? What did we invent or create? Would mankind be any the worse if we had never lived? I doubt that anyone here this evening would venture a boastful reply to these questions. We used what others invented, we enjoyed what others built. There is no Henry Ford here this evening, no Thomas Edison, no Du Pont. Our demise will perhaps be noted in some newspaper's obituary column, but not on the pages of history.

Let us turn away from this side of our lives. I have no intention to humiliate you, but I would have you feel humble. Self-perception must make us realize that we have contributed nothing to the material progress of our times which could serve as an excuse for neglect of our opportunities to further the spiritual welfare of men. Let us examine this side of our lives. We are citizens not only of the world, but also of Christ's kingdom. And here, though we be nonentities, as the world sees us, the humblest among us can make a great success of life. If you have brought one soul to eternal salvation, you did more than a general who won a battle; for the Lord assures us that one soul is more precious than all the riches of the world. In God's book of life the great are those who do His will, no matter how disparagingly the world may speak of them.

The Saviour said, "Not everyone that saith unto me Lord, Lord, shall enter into the kingdom of heaven; but he who does the will of my Father which is in heaven." He speaks not of men who know the will of the Father, or who pretend to do the will of the Father, or who intend to do the will of the Father, or who claim to do the will of the Father; no, He speaks only of those who do the will of the Father. And what it means to do the will of the Father the Saviour makes clear in our text.

This text is one of our Lord's inimitable parables, spoken in Holy Week, on the day following Palm Sunday. He had entered the temple where He was teaching, when the chief priests and the elders came to Him and rudely demanded from Him an answer, which they hoped would be a self-incrimination. "By what authority doest thou these things?" they asked, "and who gave thee this authority?" The implication of their question was, "We, the proper authorities, did not give you authority to do this; we neither ordained you as a priest nor as a preacher. You have no right to teach here in the temple."

There is hardly a parallel that equals the foolhardy tenacity with which the chief priests and elders challenged the Saviour on so many occasions. More than once I saw a dog in pursuit of a porcupine. The result was always the same. The dog found himself with a mouth full of barbed needles, which caused him to howl with pain. Deeply imbedded, they had to be extracted, one by one, with a pair of pliers. Yet, the very next day he would return to the uneven battle, which he could not win. The chief priests and elders exposed themselves to the ridicule of the people by an even greater absurdity. No matter how foolish they appeared when the Saviour exposed their sham and hypocrisy, they always came back. And so here.

The Saviour silenced them by countering with a question of His own. "The baptism of John, whence was it?" What could they say? John had no more come to them for ordination and authority than Jesus had. They well knew, if they agreed that God Himself had ordained and authorized John, He would ask, "Why did you not believe John when he pointed Me out as the Messiah?" On the other hand, if they insisted that John was not of God, the people would pounce on them; for the people still revered the memory of John. Finding no answer, they could only stand and gnash their teeth in their sheepish silliness.

Now came the parable. "A certain man had two sons; and he came to the first, and said, Son, go work today in my vineyard. He answered and said, I will not; but afterward he repented and went. And he came to the second, and said likewise. And he answered and said, I go, sir; and went not. Whether of them twain did the will of the father? They say unto him, The first. Jesus saith unto them, Verily I say unto you, That the publicans and the harlots go into the kingdom of God before you." For Him, in the presence of many people, to label the priests and elders as inferior even to publicans and harlots was a bitter pill for them to swallow. But they had asked for it.

At first we hold in admiration neither the one son, of whom the Saviour speaks in this parable, nor the other. The first, who refused to go, was guilty of disobedience and of disrespect to his father; the second who said he would go but did not go, was guilty of hypocrisy. However, the first later repented and went.

As men are by nature, none do the will of the heavenly Father. All are either outspokenly stubborn and disobedient, or they are hypocrites. Only when the Holy Spirit leads men to repentance, do they begin to do the will of the Father. Of those who first say "No" to God, some later repent. Few, however, are the hypocrites who repent. That fact compelled the Saviour to say that publicans and harlots would enter the kingdom before the chief priests and elders; for the latter were hypocrites.

It is revealing to see the reaction of people who met the Saviour personally. Among them were publicans, like Matthew and Zaccheus. The publicans had acquired a reputation for greed and dishonesty. And deservedly so. Matthew and Zaccheus, no doubt, at times despised themselves, when conscience accused them and made them feel base. Others admonished or rebuked them. However, their complete turn-about-face took place when they met Jesus, and thereby came under the influence of the Holy Spirit. The result was sincere repentance. Henceforth words and actions were motivated by the determination to do the will of the Father. Matthew became one of the twelve disciples, and Zaccheus an exemplary

Christian. Then there was the harlot, Mary Magdalena. She had been deaf to the pleadings of her parents and others to lead a decent life and to forsake the path which could only lead to ruin. Conscience must have tortured her at times. The ugly word which people attached to her must have caused her to blush with shame. But always the answer was, "No." Only when she finally met Jesus was everything changed. We are told that she loved so much because so much had been forgiven. And there were many others like her.

Seldom did hypocrites repent. The Saviour met many whose hypocrisy He unmasked, only to fan the flames of their hatred. Chief of these were the priests and elders. They wore religious garbs, differing in texture, color, and cost according to their rank. They publicized themselves as leaders of the church and servants of God. They stood in public places and uttered long prayers. They boasted of their charities while they devoured widows' houses. They reaped rich profits from the sacrifices which they instructed the people to bring to God in His holy temple. The Saviour likened them to whited sepulchers. He bluntly called them hypocrites. In the very hours when the Redeemer hung on the cross, suffering and dying for the sins of the world, offering Himself to God as the one all-sufficient Sacrifice, they went about their functions in the temple, preparing for the Passover. With the blood of the Son of God on their hands, they were deciding what to do with the blood money which the traitor had thrown at their feet before he went and hanged himself. They were busily doing the will of the devil. No wonder the Saviour said, "The publicans and harlots go into the kingdom before you." Vile criminals, like the thief on the cross, repented, but hypocrites, like the high priest, did not.

And now let us recapture our thought of a few minutes ago. Readily we admit that in the year now drawing to a close, in fact, throughout life, we contributed nothing truly noteworthy to the material progress of our generation. What about our spiritual life? All of you, who are Christians, have accomplished something. You have not only been benefited by what others did for you, but you have benefited others, otherwise you would not be Christians. Everyone here who is a Christian has been doing the will of the Father. That is the truest mark of the Christian. How much we did for God and for our fellowmen the recording angel has written into the record.

Only a hypocrite would stand and boast of his accomplishments. True Christians will only pray God to forgive what they neglected to do. Nevertheless, as an earthly father's heart thrills within him when he sees his little child bring him a cup of water, no matter how much it spills along the way, so our Heavenly Father's heart also thrills within Him when He sees His children trying to do His will.

You need not be a leader in the church to accomplish that which pleases your Father; you need never be voted into an office. Leaders and officers are often the cheapest commodity in the church, and sometimes a nuisance. The real assets of the church consist of those who in a humble and quiet way serve God and their fellowmen unobtrusively according to the ability which the Holy Spirit imparts.

Viewed in this light, this matter becomes very personal. How well did I do the will of the Father during the year fast drawing to its close? Let us not think of others; let us not compare ourselves to others. This heart-searching question is like a spotlight which we must squarely turn on ourselves. Let us not permit Satan to mislead us into any false humility or modesty. Let us thank God for having accomplished something. The Apostle wants us to thank God who made us meet to be co-workers with our Lord and Saviour in His kingdom. Many of the prayers which are read in our churches urge us to thank God for having chosen us as His servants and for having endowed us with the ability to serve Him.

On the other hand, let us not permit Satan to lead us into pride and conceit to make us think more of ourselves than we are. The danger of pride is always far greater than the danger of false modesty.

A proper self-examination on a New Year's Eve can only end with the plea, "Forgive us our trespasses" — "Blot out our transgressions." The more earnest the prayer, the clearer will be the picture of our Saviour, in whom we have plenteous forgiveness.

The calendar in our Lutheran Annual for the past year had

the first of January superscribed with the prayer — "Father, let me dedicate all this year to Thee," and for this last day of the year it suggests the prayer, "Let mercy crown our days."

In this spirit let me wish you a Happy New Year; a new year dedicated to the doing of the Father's will, for which we rely on His grace and mercy. *Amen.*

# 6

## *Once, from the East to the West; Now, from the West to the East*

### (Epiphany)
### Matthew 2:1-2

*Now when Jesus was born in Bethlehem of Judea in the days of Herod the king, behold, there came wise men from the east to Jerusalem, Saying, Where is he that is born King of the Jews? for we have seen his star in the east, and are come to worship him.*

January 6 has been a holiday in the church since the earliest days of Christianity. Originally the day commemorated the baptism of Jesus. From Jerusalem and other parts of the Holy Land Christians came to Bethabara, where John had baptized the Saviour. A service was held, the Jordan River was blessed, and then water was drawn and carried away to be used in baptisms throughout the year. Later the day was more widely celebrated as the birthday of the Lord. Today the Eastern Orthodox Church is celebrating Christmas. January 6 is called the Christmas of the gentiles. It is also called Three Kings' Day. However, here in America and in other countries also, the day commemorates the coming of the Wise Men. We call this day Epiphany Sunday, and together with the appearance of the first Gentiles before the Christ-child our thoughts are occupied with the mission work of the Christian Church among the heathen peoples of the world.

Tradition has it that the Wise Men came from Persia. It was a long journey. However, recently the Shah of Persia traveled even farther. He came all the way to America, and at about the same time our Doctor Henry Nau, in reverse, journeyed all the way to Persia, now called Iran.

The Wise Men came to Jerusalem to find the newborn King of the Jews. The Shah of Persia came here to seek financial help for his country. Dr. Nau went to Persia in the hope that our church could become instrumental in the reappearance of the star which once shone there so brightly. He went in the hope that the beginning of our church's Mohammedan Mission Work could be made there.

The Wise Men found the King in Bethlehem; the Shah found the money he sought; but Dr. Nau was not so successful. When the Wise Men came to Jerusalem, the people there were not interested in Him who was born King of the Jews. And when Dr. Nau came to Persia, he found the same disinterest.

After the fall of Babylon, Persia became the great world power. In that day of greatness Daniel and his friends, together with other Israelites in captivity, preached the hope of Israel. King Darius, as a result of his intimate association with Daniel, ordered that all lands in his great empire should worship only the true God. Later, in New Testament times, the Nestorians and other Christians, not only preached the Gospel in Persia, but firmly established the Christian Church. Now, except for a very small remnant of the Nestorian Church, Mohammedanism has occupied that entire land. It was Communism, however, which balked every effort of Dr. Nau to establish a foothold in Persia and made him turn to the Malabar Coast of India, there to begin our work among the Moslems.

There were other times when Christian missionaries found doors closed and sealed against them. When Paul, on his second missionary journey, turned toward Bithynia the Holy Spirit forbade him to go there. In God's wisdom it was not the time to begin mission work there. God had other, more fertile fields in mind.

There are times and seasons when even the most enthusiastic and ardent crusaders become very discouraged and despondent in the mission work of the church. Even Elijah was ready to give up when he sat under the juniper tree and prayed God to let him die. He no longer heard the harmonious peal of the chimes of God's wonderful promises to His Church; he heard, or thought he was hearing, the death-knell of the kingdom of God on earth.

Had Elijah in those soul-trying days trusted God's word rather than his own eyes, he would not have surrendered to so great despondency. The promises of God were clear. Again and again God had foretold that the gentiles should come to Christ and that His kingdom should be an everlasting kingdom. And in our case the Lord has foretold that the powers of hell shall not prevail against His kingdom.

When men peer into the future and foretell coming events, our own reason, judgment and common sense must govern our response and action. The Weather Bureau, for instance, issues its forecasts, and it would be folly on our part were we to ignore its prognostications; for the study of prevailing winds and temperatures does indicate future weather conditions. Experience, however, has taught us that the Weather Bureau can only draw its conclusions. It has no power to make its forecasts come true. It is an entirely different matter when God forecasts the weather. When God instructed Elijah to inform Ahab that there would be no rain for three years, there was no rain because God has the power to make His forecasts come true.

God always brings to pass what He predicts. General McArthur assured us that victory in Korea was only a matter of days, and that our men would be out of Korea by Christmas. Such was his opinion and his hope. His prediction failed because he lacked the power to verify his words. But when God told Joshua that the walls of Jericho would fall, they fell, because God had the power to make them fall.

When men foretell, our own common sense and judgment must guide our corresponding thinking and action. When God foretells, it is no longer a matter of judgment and common sense, but solely of faith. Trust in God's Word never leaves us ashamed. God foretold that the gentiles should come to Christ. There was no long delay in the fulfillment of this promise. Shortly after the Saviour's birth the Wise Men came from the East. Isaiah had foretold, "They shall bring gold and incense; and they shall show forth the praises of the Lord." And so, because God foretold it and brought it to pass, they came with their gold, frankincense, and myrrh, and knelt before the newborn King.

Their coming crazed Herod with fear, but the hearts of Joseph and Mary, Simeon and Anna, Zacharias and Elisabeth, and others were filled with joy. To them it was an earnest that God's prophesies would be fulfilled, that kings should come to His rising, and that the gentiles should worship Him. They saw the Wise Men as the vanguards of the mighty army of the Lord which should be assembled from men of all climes and places, of all races and tongues.

For our mission work we also have God's unfailing promises. Inseparable are His command to preach the Gospel and His assurance that He will be with us always. His unequivocal declaration that His Word shall not be preached in vain is always true because He makes it come true.

The holiday season has again most vividly portrayed the incarnation of the Son of God before our eyes and hearts. He, "the Wonderful Counselor, the Mighty God, the Everlasting Father, the Prince of Peace," came in poverty, in the form of a servant. This humility, which was beyond the understanding of the angels, was decreed by God in the councils of eternity, dictated by God's incomprehensible love for us lost and condemned sinners. We were the scapegallows for whom He was the scapegoat. Our sins were laid on Him, "that whosoever believeth in him shall not perish, but have everlasting life." But: "How shall they believe in him of whom they have not heard?" God asked Himself that question. As determined as He was that His Son should save all men, so determined was He that all men should hear the Gospel of salvation. And they were to hear it, not from angels, but from those who should be most eager and happy to proclaim it, from His redeemed children on earth, who have come to the light of salvation.

Love for Him in whom we have forgiveness of all of our sins, gratitude to Him who redeemed us at so great a price, pity for all who know Him not must spur us on to be about our Father's business. To our shame it must be said that we often grow dull, listless, and discouraged. We need every day to pray, "Restore unto me the joy of thy salvation." Actually we should never be discouraged. For in the end there is always victory for those who have even a grain of faith. God promised Abraham to make of him a great nation, and then commanded him to sacrifice his only son. God promised independence, glory, and power to Israel, and then seemingly forgot Jacob's children in the slavery of Egypt. God promised David a throne, and then let him become a fugitive from justice. God promised to lead the Wise Men to the newborn King, and then let them meet the crushing fact that no one in Jerusalem knew of a newborn King. But these were only temporary setbacks. God restored the joy of His salvation in all of these situations when, in the end, there came a glorious fulfillment of His promises.

We, too, must find the courage to meet with a setback now and then. We are face to face with a discouraging situation now. Communism has stretched out its iron curtain against our missionaries and has persecuted fellow Christians. But why be discouraged? Communism has not yet conquered all the world, as heathen Rome had at the time of our Saviour's earthly life. Rome could not bring the onward march of the Cross of Christ to a halt, much less will Communism be able to do so. Even now our missionaries are preaching Christ to the Chinese people in Formosa, Hong Kong and elsewhere, and in God's own time they will re-enter the mainland of China, where, I am sure, they will find many who are still true to their Lord and Saviour.

In life's darkest moments, God is nearer than we know. There came a day in the life of our Saviour when all seemed lost. Caiaphas and his cohorts were plotting to take His life. The people whom He had so wonderfully taught and healed were turning away from Him. And over all lay the shadow of the horrible, torturous cross. For Him there was no cave in which He could hide, as David did; for Him there was no juniper tree under which He could moan in solitude, as Elijah did; for Him there was no ship on which He could sail away, as Jonah did. For Him there were the certain and inescapable horrors of Gethsemane and the Cross. And what did He say in that awful hour? "Father, the hour is come; glorify thy Son, that thy Son also may glorify thee; and thou hast given him power over all flesh, that he should give eternal life to as many as thou hast given him." In the face of death He could speak of glory.

May the Holy Spirit give us Christlike eagerness to lead men to eternal life. May the Holy Spirit give us Christlike courage to meet our temporary setbacks. May He lead us, as He once led the Wise Men, to bring our gifts to the King, and to serve Him who first served us, and gave His life as a ransom for our souls. *Amen.*

# 7

## *Diversity in Unity*

### (First Sunday After Epiphany)
### Romans 12:1-8

*I beseech you therefore, brethren, by the mercies of God, that ye present your bodies a living sacrifice, holy, acceptable unto God, which is your reasonable service. And be not conformed to this world: but be yet transformed by the renewing of your mind, that ye may prove what is that good, and acceptable, and perfect, will of God. For I say, through the grace given unto me, to every man that is among you, not to think of himself more highly than he ought to think; but to think soberly, according as God hath dealt to every man the measure of faith. For as we have many members in one body, and all members have not the same office: So we, being many, are one body in Christ, and every one members one of another. Having then gifts differing according to the grace that is given to us, whether prophecy, let us prophesy according to the proportion of faith; Or ministry, let us wait on our ministering: or he that teacheth, on teaching; Or he that exhorteth, on exhortation: he that giveth, let him do it with simplicity; he that ruleth, with diligence; he that sheweth mercy, with cheerfulness.*

In this twelfth chapter of his epistle to the Romans, Paul holds before our eyes a picture of the individual congregation, and of the entire visible Church, as he sees it, and as he wants us to see it. He sees the members of the Church in their possession of a great diversity of gifts, reaching out in identical purpose to perfect an essential unity.

Any wonderful structure is the final result of a diversity of gifts aiming at perfection through unity. This is true also of any efficient machine. Two people see the latest model of an expensive automobile — say, a Cadillac or a Rolls-Royce, as it smoothly passes by. The one stands, with a drooling mouth, as he envies the occupants; the other thinks of the diversity of gifts and abilities that entered into its construction. He sees miners in Minnesota, Michigan, and Missouri producing the iron ore, copper, and zinc; he sees natives in Africa, Asia, and South America tapping trees for their latex; he sees these raw materials, in the hands of skilled labor, transformed into sheets of steel, plates of zinc, and copper wire; he sees expert mechanics building the dies which will give form to the body; he sees moulders forming the tires; he sees chemists working on the strengthening of nylon to make tires safe and durable; he sees the draftsmen bending over their boards, to design and model and to give it comfort and beauty. Now, if all these had individually tried to build an automobile, no doubt, they would have all come in ox-carts to confess their failure to each other. However, when their diversified gifts were unified in one solid purpose, the result was a Cadillac or Rolls-Royce.

Such thoughts were running through the mind of Paul when he wrote the words of the text. He compares the Church to the human body, which consists of many parts. All the parts of the body have their respective functions. There can be a sound human body only if all parts contribute to the perfection and support of the whole. Each part is indispensably necessary in the place which it occupies; and each is useful, though performing a different function.

Paul says, "So we, being many, are one body in Christ, and every one members one of another." We are members of the Church of Christ, which is considered the body of which He is the Head. We have various offices assigned to us, according to the measure of grace, faith, and religious knowledge, which has been meted out to us. Although each has a different office and qualification suitable to that office, yet all belong to that body. And the body can be hale and hearty only if each member is diligent in the performance of his office, and if the entire membership uses its diversity of gifts to build a perfect unity.

Paul here appeals to every member of the congregation to apply himself, or herself, diligently to the improvement of the office, ability, or talent, given to him, or to her, keeping modestly within its bounds, without self-exaltation and without despising others.

The Apostle mentions some of the gifts which are found in any Christian congregation: prophecy, ministry, teaching, exhorting, giving, etc. In God's endowments, which He has given to the individual congregation, there is great diversity, diversity which must aim at unity. There is the minister, who prophesies ("phophesy" here means "preach", as it so often does in the language of Scripture). When Paul in this text says, "For I say, through the grace given unto me," he does not merely mean that God endowed him with the ability to preach, but rather that God entrusted him with authority to rule over the congregation by exercising the means of grace. And since God has bestowed gifts upon all, He insists that every individual member, in one way or another, exercise his own peculiar gifts to assist the minister, to the end that the preaching of the Gospel may come to full fruition.

There is the organist. Not every organist can be a Bach. But he can make the most of the gift which God has bestowed upon him. Music has always had a major assignment in the Church of God. Think of the streams of comfort and consolation which flowed into Christian hearts from the psalms, which the sweet singer of Israel first sang to the tune of his harp. The organist who leads the Christian congregation in its songs of worship is doing that which constitutes the great delight of the saints in heaven. Luther ranked music next to theology. Let the organist to whom God has given a great talent put his heart and soul in the exercise of it, and do it to the glory of God.

Then there is teaching. Even in this one peculiar gift there is a great diversity. There is the young Christian woman who is adored by her Sunday School class, and whose one aim is to work in the Spirit of the Lord's admonition, "Suffer little children to come unto me." There is the professor of theology at the seminary, drawing on his every ability to prepare young men to preach the Gospel and to represent the Lord in the far-flung outposts of the Church's mission fields. The Christian young woman could not teach a seminary class, and the professor could not hold the attention of children. Let them stay, the one in her Sunday School, the other in his classroom. But let both be united in the one endeavor to teach the Word of God.

There is exhortation. It is, as a rule, the peculiar gift of those who have traveled the long road to old age, and who, along the way, have gathered experience, wisdom, and understanding. It is true, children can also exhort and admonish each other, and often do. Nevertheless, we do not think of exhortation as the gift of childhood. The children of the congregation have other gifts, and foremost among these, the gift of song. Nothing delights the ear and warms the heart more than the lusty voices of a children's choir. When those children sang their "Hosannas" on Palm Sunday as the Lord entered Jerusalem, His enemies protested. They could not shut their ears to the ring of sincerity; they knew the children were singing the praises of the Lord. But to Him who loved little children and said, "Let them come unto me," it was the most natural thing that they should sing as they did. He said, "If these should hold their peace, the very stones would cry out." If your child possesses the gift of song, bring it to the choir, and let it do what pleases the Lord so greatly.

On the other hand, the old, whose quivering voices can no longer be raised in song—let them be diligent in exhortation. Always their exhorting must have the one purpose of improving the Christian life of others, because it is the will of God. It must be done in humility and sincerity, free from nasty criticism or nagging, which could only serve to antagonize.

The Bible says, "A word spoken in due season, how good it is!" Many a life has been saved from utter ruin because a sympathetic and understanding Christian spoke a word of exhortation.

There is giving. Is that a Christian virtue for which only God can give us inclination and joy? I think it is. In Paul's epistles we have two quotations from the lips of Christ which are not recorded in any of the four Gospels. The one is the comforting word spoken to Paul, "My grace is sufficient for thee; for my strength is made perfect in weakness," and the other is, "It is more blessed to give than to receive." The natural unsanctified man looks upon giving as a tax which is imposed on him. By nature we are all takers rather than givers. Only God, who loves a cheerful giver, can make us cheerful givers. Here again, there is a great diversity. The poverty-stricken cannot give like millionaires. In the eyes of the world that makes a great difference, but in the eyes of God that is of no importance. God expects no poor man to give like a millionaire, but He does expect him to give like a poor man. The Apostle says, "He that giveth, let him do it with simplicity." When the newspaper photographer is called in to take a picture of a millionaire extending his check to some representative of a charity, the suspicion is immediately awakened that he is not giving with simplicity or humility.

That brings us to the important question, What should motivate us to use our peculiar gifts, of whatever nature they may be, to the one unified purpose which the Apostle has in mind?

Paul says, "I beseech you therefore, brethren, by the mercies of God, that ye present your bodies a living sacrifice, holy, acceptable unto God, which is your reasonable service." If it is your "reasonable service" to use your gifts and talents as directed in this text, then it would be unreasonable to do anything else. And unreasonable it would be. The Apostle here pictures a Christian life. If you are a Christian, such will your life be, because it is moulded thus by the Holy Spirit.

Christ said, "Without me ye can do nothing." What could we do? What could we do when we were lost in sin, unredeemed children of Satan? We could do nothing; we were blind and dead in trespasses and sins. In our helplessness God's love came to our rescue. It stopped at nothing. There was only one possible sacrifice great enough to atone for our sins. God's love made His Son a sacrifice for us. He fulfilled the law in our stead. For thirty-three years, for a generation, He lived our life to atone for our transgressions of the law by His perfect, holy life. Not enough, He brought the supreme sacrifice and laid down His life in payment for our iniquities. Could anything be more reasonable than for us to serve Him in His kingdom? It is reasonable that we should preach, worship, teach, exhort, give, and employ whatever talents we possess to show our gratitude to Him, who loved us even unto death. May the Holy Spirit make us both willing and able. *Amen.*

# 8

## *Labor Trouble Then and Now*

### (Septuagesima)
### Matthew 20:1

*For the kingdom of heaven is like unto a man that is an householder, which went out early in the morning to hire labourers into his vineyard.*

There is beauty in the words "kingdom of heaven." They bespeak perfection and holiness; harmony and peace; purity and chastity; kindliness and love. However, this chimerical picture of the kingdom of heaven is quickly marred and disfigured by the Saviour's paradoxical statement, "The Son of man shall send forth his angels, and they shall gather out of his kingdom all things that offend, and them which do iniquity." Are there such in the kingdom of heaven? Oh, yes: there are good fishes and bad; there are tares among the wheat; there are Pharisees and publicans; there are saints and harlots. People who shun the Church, claiming they know members who are hypocrites, might as well come in: there is room for more hypocrites. Such people can never say that Jesus misled them. He pictured the Church as it is.

In the Gospel for this Sunday the Saviour parabolically speaks of contented and of discontented laborers in the vineyard. Men have taught by parable since man first began to teach. But there has never been a parabolist like our Saviour. His parables are the world's masterpieces. Bruce Barton challenged scholars to add a single word to any parable of the Lord which would give it greater perfection, or to delete a single word which would not detract from its logic, clarity, and literary beauty. People, who heard His parables, said, "Never man spake as this man speaks."

This Gospel should be of special interest to us because we are all laborers. There is a fine distinction between labor and work. We distinguish the laboring class from the white-collar class. Adam would have worked even had he not sinned. He would have dressed and kept the Garden of Eden. Labor, on the other hand, painful, oppressing, depressing labor came with the fall into sin. Hard labor for life, that was God's sentence pronounced upon our exiled first parents. But the verdict was tempered by mercy. God so fashioned us and gave us such diversified gifts that we can, each in his own way, outwardly express our inward characteristics. By our labors we can supplement each other. By what we produce we can make life more tolerable and enjoyable for one another. A hundred different people have produced the hundred different articles in our homes, which have made them comfortable and enjoyable.

Only men working together can form a healthy society. Right now our port is idle, and hundreds of ships are lying at anchor with cargoes undocked, because the longshoremen have called a strike. Just before Christmas New Yorkers were greatly inconvenienced, shopping was curtailed, work was disrupted, because the subway operators tied up transportation by their strike. Next, another strike silenced our telephones. Why? It would not serve our purpose to enter upon the reasons. The results speak for themselves, laborers go without wages, management goes without profits, and the economy of the country suffers. When men do not work together, when they do not combine the talents which God has given them, everybody suffers. We are all debtors to each other, the servant to the master, capital to labor, husband to wife, neighbor to neighbor.

Moreover, we are laborers not only in this secular world; we are laborers also in the kingdom of heaven. In some respects our work in the kingdom is much like our work in our secular calling, and in other respects it is altogether different. In both cases the work is to be done. The householder went out early in the morning, and again and again during the day, to hire laborers because he wanted the work in the vineyard done. God also wants the work in the kingdom done. The most striking difference between our twin callings comes at the end of day, when we find that in the kingdom we have earned nothing. In the kingdom of heaven, strictly speaking, no one can earn anything. All we have ever earned is damnation, and if we escape damnation it is entirely due to God's grace, and not to anything we have done. Here the word of the Saviour applies, "When ye have done all these things, say, we are unprofitable servants."

There are always people who speak of their earnings in the Lord's vineyard. They do things, and they expect pay. For services rendered they insist on a corresponding amount of forgiveness. The new Catholic Bible promises forgiveness for a certain number of days to all who kiss the Bible daily. Convinced that unpardoned sins must be paid for in purgatory, misguided souls seek to shorten their stay in the dread abode by earning as much forgiveness as possible.

The Lord has something to say about this in the parable of the laborers. Some workmen insisted they had earned more than others who had put in less time. As usual, they found their spokesman, their union leader, who voiced their grievances. But the householder quickly silenced him. "Didst not thou agree with me for a penny?" he asked. The words implied, "You insisted on a contract. Did I not pay you according to the contract? You bargained, and I kept the bargain. These others trusted me. They believed me when I said I would be fair. Now, when I pay them as much as I pay you, do I not have a right to do so?" The murmurers were not so much disgruntled with the small amount they had earned, as they were with the large amount the others received. Their eyes were evil. Their hearts were jealous. Humble workers in the Lord's vineyard, seeking only to serve God and their fellow men, will receive a reward of grace far beyond their expectations, and those who think God owes them much for what they have done will be bitterly disillusioned.

The first to enter the vineyard in the morning agreed to work all day for a penny. That sounds like small pay; and it was. Nevertheless, it was in accordance with the wage standard of the time. In England, in the year 1351, a wage scale was established by parliament. Corn-hoers and hay-makers (in other words, farmhands), like the laborers in the vineyard, were to be paid one penny a day. Small pay! Yes, but people could live on it; for eggs sold twenty-four for a penny, a goose for two and a half pennies, a hen for a penny. I suppose that the scene in the vineyard was repeated then also. When, in the busy season of the harvest, men worked part of a day, a kindly English householder may also have paid them a full penny, thus giving more than laborers had a right to expect.

It goes without saying that in the Saviour's day, as well as in England in the fourteenth century, a penny was the pay for unskilled labor. And that is exactly the point which the Saviour makes here; for in the kingdom of heaven we are all unskilled laborers. The Saviour said, "Without me ye can do nothing." Of ourselves, we cannot even enter the vineyard. I believe that I cannot by my own reason or strength come to Him. The Holy Ghost has to call us, and He has to enlighten us so that we can find the entrance. There can, therefore, be no earning; the only possible reward is one of grace, and not of merit.

Let us be mindful of the fact that the Lord here speaks only of men who entered the vineyard, and worked. No doubt, as the householder went forth to hire laborers, some refused his offer. They did not come into the vineyard. They are not mentioned here, Naturally, they received no consideration when the householder paid the laborers. Millions refuse God's gracious invitation to come into the Church. Of such the Saviour does not speak here. For such there is only damnation. The Lord speaks only of those who are in the Church. Of these, some, like Samuel and John the Baptist, were dedicated to the Lord's service even before they were born. Some, like Timothy, are the Lord's own since childhood. Some, like

Andrew and Nathanael, may become special servants of the Lord in early manhood, and serve Him with faithfulness and humility. Others, like James and Peter, may come later, but accomplish more. Still others, like Paul, may come much later, but serve with far greater distinction. Others, having no special calling, like Lazarus, Martha, the Galilean women who followed Him, may manifest their love for Him in a thousand different ways.

"Many are called, but few are chosen." Of those whom the Holy Ghost calls into the kingdom, only a few are chosen to serve the Lord in a special calling. Paul said, "Not many mighty are called." Paul, a Roman citizen, was probably thinking of the Roman army when he wrote these words. Rome did not force men to serve in its army; for to serve was considered a great honor. All were called, not many were chosen. All boys were trained for the army from youth. They were taught to run, to leap, to swim, to wrestle, to throw the javelin, to carry heavy burdens, and to march for hours on end. Each year twenty-four tribunes were chosen to cammand the four legions. Then the people, according to tribes, presented their men to the tribunes, some to be selected as officers, others to serve in the ranks. That left unchosen the great majority of all who were called, trained, and presented. These served the empire in a less spectacular, though sometimes more faithful, manner.

Thus in the kingdom of heaven. Some are chosen to serve in a spectacular manner. Not many, however. Only a few reach the stature of Paul, Peter, Luther, and a handful of others. The great, great majority serve in a far humbler capacity. But of these, some may be more highly honored by the Lord than many others, because their love for Him is greater.

If we can earn nothing in the kingdom, then it again comes down to this—that we are saved alone by grace, and not by works. We shall not enter upon the old objection, "You Lutherans teach it matters not if a man can show no good works, if he believes." The argument is too shallow to deserve an answer. Where there is true faith, there will be good works as surely as a good tree will bear good fruit. A man who was being ferried across a stream noticed that the ferryman's one oar was inscribed with the word "faith," and the other with the word "works." Asked for the reason, he replied, "Let me demonstrate." He pulled only with one oar, and the boat turned in circles, then he pulled only with the other oar, and the boat circled in the opposite direction. When, however, he pulled with both oars the boat held a straight course. May the Holy Spirit help us to pull with both oars. *Amen.*

# 9

## *A Living Epistle to a Living Congregation*

### (Second Sunday in Lent)
Thessalonians 1:2-3

*We give thanks to God always for you all, making mention of you in our prayers; Remembering without ceasing your work of faith, and labour of love and patience of hope in our Lord Jesus Christ, in the sight of God and our Father.*

The Scripture passage which is customarily read on this second Sunday in Lent is taken from the fourth chapter of Paul's first letter to the Thessalonians. Today, however, I have chosen a sentence from the first chapter, an informative word, which opens up an insight into the life of the Church at Thessalonike.

Within a year Paul addressed two letters to the Thessalonians. They attract our interest because they were the first of his great epistles. They were written during Paul's stay in Corinth. Here, then, we have the beginning of Christian literature.

Men attach a great deal of sentiment and of importance to a first edition, and especially to the first copy of a first edition, which is generally presented to the author. Original manuscripts have brought fabulous prices. Any financial worries which you may have would quickly be dissipated if you could come upon the original of Paul's first epistle to the Thessalonians; all the more so because you would in that case also have Paul's autograph; for he signed it with his own hand.

The second epistle ends with the sentence, "The salutation of Paul with mine own hand, which is the token of every epistle." Undoubtedly, Paul wrote and dictated many letters, which were not divinely inspired, and, therefore, do not form a part of the New Testament. Always he signed his letters with his own hand. As it developed later, false teachers also wrote letters to the Christian congregations. Some may even have resorted to forgery, necessitating Paul's precaution in appending his signature, especially to divinely inspired epistles

As has been said, in this epistle we have the beginning of Christian literature. Millions and millions of words have been added during the centuries, some excellent, far more mere trash. No one, since those early days, has produced anything comparable to Paul's epistles, for the simple reason that his writings were divinely inspired.

The two epistles to the Thessalonians should interest us greatly for three reasons. One has already been mentioned. They were the first. The second quickly followed the first. Paul had received glowing reports on conditions in Thessalonike, which spoke of the sincerity and steadfastness of the members. On one point, however, they were in need of enlightenment. Somehow they had gained the impression that Paul and the other apostles were divinely assured that the judgment day would come during their lifetime. To correct this erroneous assumption, Paul immediately addressed another epistle to them.

The second appeal to our interest in these epistles rests on the fact that they were written to an excellent congregation. Paul's epistles always disclose the state of affairs in the congregations to whom they are addressed. His letters to the Corinthians, for instance, and to the Galatians express severe criticism and condemnation. The Galatians had permitted false teachers to lead them back under the yoke of the Old Testament ceremonial law; and the Corinthians had grown indifferent, permitting gross immorality to exist in the congregation. The Thessalonians were not guilty of such misconduct. Except for the one false impression under which they labored, Paul had no fault to find. On the contrary, he assured them that he always thanked God for them and remembered them in his prayers. He lauded their "work of faith, and labor of love, and patience of hope."

These words are worthy of consideration and study by every Christian congregation. When Paul came to Thessalonike, he found three classes of people; namely, Jews; devout Greeks, that is Greeks who had been converted to the Jewish faith, or who, though of Jewish blood, had been born in Macedonia; and finally, out-and-out heathen. As elsewhere so here; the Jews turned against Paul. It was the old bugaboo; they rebelled against the suggestion that they should admit gentiles and accept them as equals without submitting to circumcision, and without abstaining from foods which were unclean to the Jew. The devout Greeks, on the other hand, and the converted gentiles received Paul with gladness, and soon blossomed forth in a flourishing congregation. The Jews answered in their accustomed manner. They resorted to persecution. In the Acts we read, "They took unto them certain lewd fellows of the baser sort." In other words, they hired hoodlums and jail birds to stage a riot. They stormed the house of Jason, where Paul and Silas resided, and when they did not find them, they dragged Jason and others from the house and took them to the magistrates, where, not the hoodlums, but the Christians were compelled to post bonds to keep the peace. When Paul could no longer stay, Silas and Timothy ministered unto the congregation.

From his fellow workers, Silas and Timothy, Paul received the report of faith and virtue in Thessalonike. The result was his first epistle, in which he commended the Christians for their work of faith, labor of love, and patience of hope. Theirs was a faith that worked. While the faith of false Christians is dead, the faith of true Christians always works. The faith that works produces the desired results. It not only leads to final salvation, which is the end and aim of faith, but it makes its presence known in the community, in the state, and in the nation. Paul acknowledged that the labor of love of the Thessalonians went out to all the brethren in Macedonia. The sick were administered to, the hungry were fed, the desolate were comforted. The outlet of their working faith was their labor of love.

With the coming of Christianity the Thessalonians had learned something entirely new. As the heathen always do, they had feared their gods and had lived in terror of their spite. Some time ago, on television, a paleontologist showed a human skull, more than a thousand years old, discovered in South America. It clearly showed that an operation had been performed on it and that it had been opened. Such operations were common also in Egypt and other ancient countries. A persistent headache, or some form of insanity, was accepted as the work of some spiteful god who had confined an evil spirit in the skull of the patient. And so the skull was opened to permit the evil spirit to escape. The crude operation almost always ended in death. But greater than the fear of death was the anxiety to escape from the hatred and spite of an evil god. The Thessalonians had likewise lived in dread of their gods. But now they had heard the Gospel. They learned that, far from hating them, "God so loved the world that he gave his only begotten Son, that whosoever believeth in him should not perish, but have everlasting life." Now they knew themselves to be fully and completely justified by faith in Christ, who had died to save them from their sins, and had made them children of God, and heirs of everlasting life. Death was no longer the monster which it had been, and judgment day was eagerly and joyfully awaited. They felt the inner compulsion to love others, because God had first loved them. And with their working faith and laboring love went patience and hope. Assured of their final delivery in eternal life they could patiently endure tribulations and persecution, knowing that they were in the hands of their loving Saviour.

This is the second reason for our interest in this epistle. It gives us an insight into the life of a wonderful congregation.

And what must be of great interest, in the third place, is the lesson contained in this epistle for us in these troublesome times.

Thessalonike, or Salonica, as it is called today, is still a great city, with a population of about 240,000 people. Many other great cities in which Paul labored are destroyed, or only a shadow of their former selves. Salonica is still an important city. And who can gainsay the Christian conclusion that it is what it is because God blessed it for what it once was? From the year 52 when Paul wrote this epistle to our day there was never a time in which there was no Christian Church in Salonica. We know that God would have spared Sodom if ten righteous people had been found in it. We know that Capernaum was utterly destroyed because it rejected the great grace which God had bestowed upon it. Why should we doubt that Salonica was spared only because its people accepted the love and grace of God?

We are confronted with a death struggle between democracy and Communism. And there are times when we are afraid. Why should we be? Communism denies the existence of God, and, therefore, Communism will destroy itself. The Bible says, "The fool hath said in his heart, there is no God." Communists are fools. God says so. Recently men in our own country voiced a protest against religious scenes on television, which, they say, "are an offense to atheists." The Bible has a different name for them. Religion is an offense only to fools. A fool is a fool. Fools do not build anything that is lasting and abiding. The world has had many Stalins and Hitlers of greater intelligence than the upstarts who are now strutting upon the scene. They destroyed themselves because they branded themselves as fools when they denied the existence of God.

However, let that not only be a comfort to us; let it also serve us as a warning. Let us be sure that we are building that which is lasting and abiding. "Righteousness exalteth a nation." National righteousness can only come through Christians with a faith that works, a love that labors, and a hope that is patient.

May God give us Christian congregations that pattern after the congregation in Thessalonike, and may God give our congregation grace to be and remain a true flock of Christ, so that its influence for good stretch out far and wide, working that which is pleasing to God. *Amen.*

# 10

## *The King Enters, Knowing the Cross Awaits Him*

### (Palm Sunday)
### Matthew 21:5

*Tell ye the daughter of Sion, Behold, thy King cometh unto thee, meek, and sitting upon an ass, and a colt the foal of an ass.*

Ever since there have been sovereigns and subjects, kings have fled before their would-be murderers. Far back in history, in the days of Abraham, the kings of Sodom and Gomorrah fled to the slimepits in the valley of Siddim, where they were slain. David escaped when he fled before Absalom, but the memory of his son's treachery became an abiding sorrow. Louis XVI and his queen, Marie Antoinette, lost their royal heads when their flight ended in their capture. Even in our day, when only a few kings remain, some, having successfully escaped the wrath of their subjects, are living in exile. Many kings have fled. Only one, and He the King of kings, entered His royal city, determined to meet His enemies with the avowed purpose of being murdered by them. He is our Lord and Saviour, Jesus Christ.

He entered Jerusalem as Israel's King. As such the people recognized Him and acclaimed Him. They spread out their

garments before Him. That was a deference reserved only
for a king. When Jehu, having been anointed king by the
prophet, Elisha, came out of the chamber into which the
prophet had taken him to anoint him, "every man took his
garment, and spread it under him on the top of the steps,"
saying, "Jehu is king."

The people shout, "Hosanna to the son of David!" "Hosanna" means, "help us," "save us." This also had long ago
become the customary manner in which subjects petitioned
their king. In II Samuel 14:4 we read that a woman, appearing
before David the king, used the same salutation. Again, in
II Kings 6:26 we read, "And as the king of Israel was passing
by upon the wall, there cried a woman unto him, saying, Help,
my Lord, O king." Thus the psalmist, looking forward to the
day of the Messiah, cried, "Save now, I beseech thee, O Lord."
By spreading their garments before Him and by shouting,
"Hosanna to the son of David," the people witnessed that
they recognized Him as their King, the promised Messiah.

On that Palm Sunday Jesus could have entered upon one
of two courses of action which were open to Him. He could
have called upon the people to arm themselves and to fight
against oppression. Unquestionably, by evening, Caiaphas,
Pilate, and Herod could all have been dead and He could
have been enthroned. On the other hand, He could have escaped. Only a few days earlier His enemies had picked up
stones to hurl at Him, but found no target.

But He did neither. He went on to be murdered that His
people might live. The cry of the people was, "Long live
the King"; His, "Let the King perish; long live the people."

Christ's entrance into Jerusalem on Palm Sunday has been
called His triumph. For the people of that day it was not
a new thing. Rome had frequently staged a triumph. Such was
the pageant of the entry of a victorious consul, dictator, or
praetor into Rome, given only for a decisive victory over a
foreign enemy. Thus even in our day Paris has its Arch of
Triumph, through which its victorious armies entered in the
heyday of France's greatness. As I write these words, newspapers and radios are reporting the triumphal entry of the
rebel Fidel Castro into Havana. And for our Lord it was,

indeed, a triumph; but it was the triumph of humility over pride and worldly grandeur; of poverty over affluence; of meekness and gentleness over rage and malice.

Had this been the entry of a rabble-rouser, Pilate would not have been so perplexed. He knew how to deal with rebels and would-be kings. He knew this was not the kind of a king Rome had reason to fear. There was more astonishment than incredulity in his question, "Art thou then a king?" He realized that Jesus could be a king, a great king, but he knew that the Accused was not such a king as His enemies represented Him to be.

On the other hand, had He entered Jerusalem as a worldly Messiah, Caiaphas might have welcomed Him. Then it might have been Caiaphas who sought to have Him released; for, like every Jew, he hated Roman oppression. As it was, Pilate would gladly have acquitted Him, fearing that He was far more than a mere king, while Caiaphas was determined to slay Him because he knew Him to be far more than a king.

It was man's blind and stubborn opposition to God's gracious will that turned triumph into tragedy. Caiaphas and his cohorts were not interested in the fall of Satan's fortress, but in the end of Rome's rule. A Saviour was not welcome.

When He entered Jerusalem, as we read in the words following today's Gospel, "the city was moved." The populace was aroused. There was great excitement. The people asked, "Who is this?" And His loyal followers answered. "This is Jesus the prophet of Nazareth of Galilee." They had greeted Him and acclaimed Him as a king, but to them He was more. They had long waited for the "prophet after the order of Melchizedek." As such He was greeted by those who believed on Him. As such He was condemned by the leaders.

What happened in Jerusalem on that Palm Sunday is of vital importance to us, because the situation is unchanged. Now as then, the great majority is ready to welcome Him as anything but what He claims to be, the Son of God and the Saviour of the world. He is welcome in any Moslem mosque, so long as He comes as a prophet and not as the prophet. Islam accepts Him as a prophet, even as a great prophet, but not as the equal of Mohammed.

He is welcome in any Christian Science temple as long as He comes as a healer of the body, and not a healer of the soul. Salvation by the sacrifice of His blood, said Mary Baker Eddy, is a loathsome doctrine.

He is welcome in the Vatican, so long as He does not claim that men are saved alone by faith in Him. Caiaphas insisted that the traditions of the elders were of equal authority with the Word of God. The pope makes the same claims for his decrees. Christ may rule in heaven, so long as He lets the pope rule on earth.

He is welcome in the halls of great universities, so long as He comes as a teacher, and not as the Saviour. He is not welcome in Jewish synagogues because they at least know, as their fathers knew, that if they cannot live with Him as the Saviour from sin, then they cannot live with Him at all, and must crucify Him.

Today the question which is posed before us is, "How do we accept Him?" "Behold, I stand at the door, and knock." Are we ready to bid Him enter? If so, then our acceptance of Him must be without reservation. It must be a complete surrender to Him. There can be no halfway measures. The cowardice of Pilate was ugly; the envy and hate of Caiaphas was uglier; but ugliest of all was the feigned friendship and hypocrisy of Judas. Over against Jesus it must be all or nothing.

Today our plea must be, "Hosanna — save us." We need saving. For, left to ourselves, we are sinners. "There is not a just man upon earth"; that is an all-embracing condemnation. Our inborn sinfulness shuts us off from any access to the Father and to eternal life. "The soul that sinneth, it shall die." We could not shed sin. To the very core of our being we are sinners, sinners in thought, word, and deed. Sin murdered Him; our sin slew Him. But His great, unbelievably great, love could not see us die eternally without a supreme effort on His part to save us. He voluntarily entered Jerusalem, knowing full well what was in store for Him.

He is our only Saviour. As such He comes today. Let us confess our sinfulness, and hail His love and mercy. May the Holy Spirit grant us grace to put sincerity, joy, and complete surrender into our plea, "Hosanna — Lord, save us." *Amen.*

*The following seven sermonettes, based on the Saviour's Seven Words from the Cross, were preached in various Baltimore churches in the customary Three-Hour Services, on Good Friday afternoons. In these services each sermonette is, as a rule, preceded by a hymn, and the reading of a part of the passion history, or some appropriate portion of Holy Writ. Each section of the Three-Hour Service is closed with prayer, and the entire service is concluded with the benediction.*

# 11

## Condemned for the Sins of Men, He Prays for Their Pardon

### (The First Word)
### Luke 23:34

*Then said Jesus, Father, forgive them; for they know not what they do. And they parted his raiment, and cast lots.*

It is nine o'clock in the morning of Good Friday. Our Lord, the Son of God, has just been crucified. Judging by outward appearance He is anyone but the Son of God. The Cross, to us so endearing and comforting, is to the eye-witnesses as ugly and repulsive as the hangman's rope or the electric chair is to the people of our day. He hangs between two thieves, and it requires more than Pilate's superscription, nailed to the cross, to distinguish Him from the transgressors who share His fate. The superscription reads, "Jesus of Nazareth, King of the Jews." No one believes it. God had on two occasions hung His own superscription in the skies. It read, "This is my beloved Son." No one believed that. Before the day was over some smote on their breasts and returned. Now they knew.

Only once during our Saviour's earthly life did His personal appearance lend conviction to His claim that He is the

Son of God; namely on the Mount of Transfiguration. Men's faith was not to depend on their own eyesight but on the unfailing Word of God. Christ was to be recognized as the Messiah, not so much by His miracles as by the fact that He and He alone, fulfilled all Scripture. His whole life was a fulfillment of Scripture. But now, in His final moments, prophecy after prophecy, as if afraid of being too late, was rushing toward its fulfillment. That He should be lifted up, as Moses lifted up a serpent in the wilderness; that He should be numbered among the transgressors, as now He was, hanging between two thieves; that they should divide His garments among them, as they now did; that of Him not a bone should be broken, as His bones were not broken when those of the thieves were; that they should see Him whom they pierced, as was done when the soldiers opened His side with a spear — these and other incidents corroborated His words, "The scriptures cannot be broken."

The marvelous fifty-third chapter of Isaiah, which reads as if the writer had stood under the cross and had witnessed all the events of Good Friday, closes with the words, "and made intercession for the transgressors."

Men were accustomed to hear only cries of pain and vile language from the lips of crucified criminals. This was something entirely new. No sooner was the cross jolted into its earthy socket when words of prayer were heard, the words of a most unusual prayer. Our Saviour does not pray for forgiveness of His own sins. He, the sinless one, had no sins to be forgiven. He does not say, "Father, I forgive you for what you are doing to Me"; He knew that this was divine justice at its highest. No, He is praying for His crucifiers. "Father, forgive them, for they know not what they do."

He came as the High Priest after the order of Melchizedek. The divinely appointed functions of the high priest were to sacrifice and to make intercession for the people. Now the great High Priest, whom all other high priests had merely foreshadowed, the one Mediator between God and men, hung between heaven and earth. Now, as the true High Priest sent from heaven, He was bringing the one all-atoning sacrifice for the sins of all the world. Now, as the great Intercessor, He prayed.

"Father, forgive them, for they know not what they do." They knew that they were crucifying an innocent man. However, they did not know that they were sealing the doom of their great temple and city. They did not know that by their action they condemned their children to become an accursed race, hated and enslaved. They did not know that for centuries to come their offspring would be the "wandering Jew." These things they did not know; nor did they in their blindness know that they were crucifying their Saviour, the Son of God. Already six days earlier, standing on the Mount of Olives, on Palm Sunday, He had said, "If thou hadst known, even thou, at least in this thy day, the things which belong unto thy peace! but now they are hid from thine eyes."

For us this is a mighty comfort that our Saviour, even on the cross, prayed for us, His crucifiers. Those Good Friday crucifiers were only the servants of our sins. They were doing our will, as it is by nature. We, by our sins, crowned Him with thorns and crucified Him. Like a sound wave from the strongest transmitter, His prayer spread out until it covered and embraced all men; for all have sinned. That was the purpose of His coming — to forgive.

He prayed! Father, I am a man, I have brothers and sisters. They are enmeshed by sin and in danger of death and hell. I am dying for them. Accept this sacrifice and be merciful to forgive all their sins. It was a pleasant sound in the ear of our heavenly Father; for thereto had He sent Him, as the sacrificial Lamb to atone for our sins.

In His love He is still our High Priest, and He is still interceding for us before the throne of God. May our prayer for forgiveness be joined to His, until prayer becomes praise in everlasting glory. *Amen.*

# 12

## *The Crucified Thief's Cross Became a Stepping Stone*

### (The Second Word)
#### Luke 23:42-43

*And he said unto Jesus, Lord, remember me when thou comest into thy kingdom. And Jesus said unto him, Verily I say unto thee, Today shalt thou be with me in paradise.*

The history of our Lord is full of the unexpected. He Himself, the King of kings, is born in a stable. As assistants in His mission to establish an everlasting kingdom He selected men from the humblest walks of life. One moment He kneels in the dust of a cemetery, tears rolling down His cheeks, portraying the acme of helpless grief, and the next moment He stands, His face radiating His majesty, and commands the body of Lazarus, already in the grip of decomposition, to come forth from the grave. He finds greater faith in the heart of a gentile, a Roman centurion, than in the Jewish high priest. And now, hanging on the cross, He finds the first one of the great company of the redeemed who were to believe on Him in His death. And He finds him in the most unlikely place, on the adjacent cross.

A few days before His crucifixion the Saviour said, "And I, if I be lifted up from the earth, will draw all men unto me." And here comes the first one, a dying thief. Three hours later came the second. This time it was a gentile, the centurion, who had given the order to nail Him to the cross. On Easter morning came the third, Mary Magdalena, who had been a harlot. What a vanguard! A thief, a heathen, a harlot. By Easter Sunday evening His disciples again were loyal. A few weeks later there were five hundred on a mountain top. On Pentecost there were three thousand. A week later there were five thousand. The cross was exerting its drawing power.

How did this twelfth-hour convert, the thief on the cross, come to faith? Only one thing we know of a certainty, the rest is conjecture. We know that he had heard of Jesus; for "faith cometh by hearing." Evidently he was a Jew, for Roman citizens were not crucified. As a Jewish boy he may have had godly parents who spoke of the coming Messiah. In the synagogue he may have become acquainted with the prophecies. And now in all the bedlam and mockery and cursing he had heard Him pray, 'Father, forgive them, for they know not what they do." If God was His father, then He must be the Son of God. At any rate, by the miraculous power of the Holy Ghost, he was enabled to see what was hidden from the eyes of all the others. Perhaps he had been in Pilate's court that morning when Jesus said, "My kingdom is not of this world." Yes, the Messiah was to build an "everlasting kingdom." And so he prayed, "Lord, remember me when thou cometh into thy kingdom."

When the psalmist had foretold, "Thy kingdom is an everlasting kingdom, and thy dominion endureth throughout all generations," he never envisioned this crucifixion scene. Here is the King and one of the first subjects of the new kingdom. Both have been excommunicated by their church; both have been condemned by their government; and within a few hours both will have died a felon's death. Who would expect the one to say to the other, "Verily, I say unto thee, Today shalt thou be with me in Paradise"? It is one of the most beautiful and comforting words in the Gospel.

Only Christ, the author and the heart of the Gospel, could

have said, "Verily, I say unto thee, today shalt thou be with me in paradise." Every other religion has a mere teacher, but the Christian religion has a Saviour. He came to save men, all men, from their sins, from all sins.

Thank God for the comfort of this word from the cross. Sinners all, all need forgiveness. The only unforgiven are those who feel no need for forgiveness. Later that day, when our Lord's body was taken to the grave, our sins were buried with Him. He did not bring them with Him when He came forth from the grace. He left them there. Let us not dig them up again. In our Lutheran Hymnal we have a choral based on the Gospel of the prodigal son. We sing:

> Redeemed, restored, forgiven
> Through Jesus' precious blood,
> Heirs of His home in heaven,
> Oh, praise our pard'ning God.

Yes, "redeemed, restored, forgiven." Let us leave it that way; let us, in the knowledge that our sins are forgiven, confidently await our glorious "today," when He shall say to us, "Verily, I say unto thee, today shalt thou be with me in paradise." *Amen.*

# 13

## Mother and Son at the Parting of the Ways

### (The Third Word)
### John 19:26-27

*When Jesus therefore saw his mother, and the disciple standing by, whom he loved, he saith unto his mother, Woman, behold thy son! Then saith he to the disciple, Behold thy mother! And from that hour that disciple took her unto his own home.*

Great crosses, overlaid with gold, on the spires of cathedrals; great crosses of marble on mountain-tops; crosses, multiplied like the trees of the forest, in cemeteries; crosses of precious metals, and studded with gems, worn as ornaments — all these have somewhat taken the ugliness out of the crosses, on which men once paid for their crimes with their lives.

It was the holy, innocent Christ who transformed the cross, once the symbol of guilt and shame, into a symbol of redemption and glory. Seven times the Saviour spoke, and His seven words made the accursed three serve as a setting for priceless gems. It is our great High Priest who makes intercession and prays, "Father, forgive them; for they know not what they do." It is the King of kings, extending a divine pardon, who says,

"Verily, I say unto thee, thou today shalt be with me in paradise." It is the Son of God, who addresses the almighty Creator as "Father." It is the Son of man, who provides for His mother, and says, "Woman, behold thy son."

From the dawn of creation until now, there has never been such an outpouring of hate as was manifested on Good Friday. No wonder! It was the fiendish hate of Satan, who personifies all the hate of hell, which, wave after wave, smashed against the Rock of Ages. Nor has there from the dawn of creation until now been such an outpouring of love as was manifested on Good Friday. No wonder! It was the divine, eternal love of God, which lifted itself to its highest peak.

John, the beloved disciple, wrote, "Having loved his own which were in the world, he loved them unto the end." He knew, for in the final moments of the Saviour's life he stood under the cross, with the Saviour's mother leaning on his arm, and saw one more gesture of the Redeemer's abiding love.

Human words cannot picture the conflict between faith and doubt, which raged in Mary's heart. Had her faith stood the test, nothing would have kept her from the tomb on Easter morning when her friends went out there to embalm a corpse. But she did not go. The death of her son left her too grief-stricken. As Simeon had foretold, a sword pierced her soul.

As Jesus looked down on her, His arms could not take her in a final embrace, but His love could. Looking from Mary to John, He said, "Woman, behold thy son," and to John He said, "Behold thy mother." Clearly His words meant, "Thou shalt not be forsaken; for My friend, who is now at thy side, shall remain at thy side, and provide for thee." John was to be a son to her, as she was to be a mother to him.

If there were no other evidences that Mary was a poor, sinful human being, like all other men, this scene alone would expose the entire Mariolatry that is practiced in the papal church, and would explode the ugly idolatry with which the last pope encumbered his followers when he ordered that the bodily assumption into heaven must be accepted as an article of faith. The Bible declares "there is one mediator between God and man, the man, Christ Jesus." Had God intended that there should be another, then Christ would have instructed

John henceforth to worship Mary as the queen of heaven. Instead, He had pity on her helplessness and asked John to provide for her.

But let us turn away from the unbiblical Mariolatry of the papists, to the real beauty of the scene. "Woman, behold thy son." "Woman." There was no more disrespect implied than when in our day a prince calls his royal father or mother, "Sir" or "Madam." But why did He not call her mother? Once before He had called her, "Woman"; namely, at the wedding of Cana, when she overstepped the bound of her relationship to Him and ventured to tell Him what to do in His Messianic ministry. Now He addresses her as "Woman," because her earthly relationship to Him had come to an end. But His love for her continued, and in the exercise of it He now provided her with another son to take the place of Himself who no longer stood in the same relationship to her. Henceforth He was only her Saviour and Redeemer, as He is Saviour and Redeemer of all.

When our Lord provides, He provides. Of all His disciples, only John did not suffer a martyr's death, but lived to an old age. The Saviour granted him a long life to enable him to perform the loving service to the Saviour's mother, which He here imposed on him. Thus God has a thousand times since then granted children long life and prosperity to the end that they might provide for their parents in their old age. Thus He still provides through old age as He once provided for Mary.

May the Holy Spirit help us to see this third word as one of the gems on the cross of Christ, so that more and more we may behold its beauty and the glory of Him who was crucified to atone for our sins. *Amen.*

# 14

## The Cry of the Damned—May We Never Hear It

### (The Fourth Word)
#### Matthew 27:46

*And about the ninth hour Jesus cried with a loud voice, saying, Eli, Eli, lama sa-bach-thani? that is to say, My God, my God, why hast thou forsaken me?*

It was high noon. The Saviour who was crucified at nine o'clock in the morning had now reached the halfway mark of His suffering upon the cross. The soldiers had divided His garments among them, and the fall of the dice had determined the winner of His coat "which was without seam, woven from the top throughout." Had the soldiers known that in the years to come relic hunters and idolators would be willing to pay a fabulous price for that coat, they would have put even more zest into their dicing. The people surrounding the cross, who did not know what they were doing, were still cursing Him and mocking Him.

And now, without warning, nature played a most terrifying role in that scene. The sun was shrouded, and darkness covered all the earth. The Passover was celebrated only at the full moon, a time in which it was impossible for the sun to be eclipsed. This was far more than a mere phenomenon. This was an act of God. In ancient writings of Egypt and other countries mention is made of a darkness that covered all the earth. Whether this darkness is referred to, we do not know. For us it is enough that the Word of God tells us, "Now from the sixth hour, there was darkness over all the land."

Critics have freely discussed God's intent in causing this miraculous darkness. Some have said it should have caused the enemies of Christ to understand that He was the light of the world and that, because they did not walk in it, it was now taken away from them. Many have failed to understand the much deeper meaning of the darkness. It can be rightly explained only by those who understand the Saviour's fourth word from the cross.

Out of the darkness came the most terrible outcry this world has ever heard, "My God, my God, why hast thou forsaken me?" Forsaken of God, that in the fullest sense is the torture of hell. And now the Saviour was suffering hell, the agony of the damned. It was the price He had to pay. In no other way could we be saved.

God does not and cannot say one thing today and the opposite tomorrow. His holiness and justice did not permit Him to retract His judgment, "The soul that sinneth it shall die." All were sinners, and therefore all were condemned to death, to hell and damnation. Either we had to suffer hell, or the Son of God had to suffer hell for us. "There is salvation in none other."

"Why hast thou forsaken me?" Only in hell are men ever, entirely and everlastingly, forsaken of God. In hell is no grace of God, not a glimmer of hope, only darkness, weeping and gnashing of teeth. All the damned in hell see is God's wrath and vengeance. Satan, his fiendish angels, the eternally accursed, that is hell.

Hell, that is what our Lord was now suffering. No mortal eye on this earth has ever seen the tortures of hell. On this earth, no man, as long as he still draws a breath, is forsaken of God. Even Judas was not forsaken of God until the rope finally choked out his miserable life. But our Lord, our substitute, was forsaken of God, suffering the agonies of hell.

God did not want any man to see that. God never intended

that any man should see the tortures of hell. The only place you could ever be forsaken of God, the only place you could ever see hell, is in hell. That was God's purpose in covering the earth with dense darkness on that Good Friday. In this world no one was to see what God intended no man ever to see.

But even now, though He was forsaken of God, He did not forsake God. He still cries, "My God, my God!" No one in hell ever says, "My God." There God is only hated and cursed. Jesus is still the holy, innocent Lamb of God. It was our punishment He endured.

Oh, what a comfort that now we will never have reason to say, "My God, my God, why hast thou forsaken me?" Since Christ spoke these words, we have no reason to repeat them. In one of our wonderful Lutheran chorals we sing, "O God, forsake me not," but we add the words, "Lord, I am Thine forever." Christ made us forever redeemed children of God.

"God so loved the world that he gave his only begotten Son." God's love for us poor sinners was so great that He condemned His own Son to suffer the agonies of the damned for us. But during those long hours God was longing for, and looking forward to, the hour when He could again show His friendly and loving face to His Son. And today we see only His kind and loving face, and know that not hell, but heaven is our home. This we owe to Jesus, "Thousand, thousand thanks shall be, dearest Jesus, unto Thee." *Amen.*

# 15

## *For Him—Agonizing Thirst; for Us— Living Waters*

### (The Fifth Word)
### John 19:28

*After this, Jesus knowing that all things were now accomplished, that the scripture might be fulfilled, saith, I thirst.*

When the Saviour had reached Golgotha and was about to be crucified, "they gave him vinegar to drink mingled with gall." This was an opiate, intended to lessen somewhat the excruciating pain of the cross. But He refused to drink it.

In the Garden of Gethsemane our Redeemer pleaded with His Father to remove the cup from Him. In answer an angel was sent from heaven to strengthen Him, again to remind Him that there was no other way to redeem fallen mankind. From there He went forth with renewed determination to drink the bitter cup to its very dregs. He wanted no opiate to dilute the contents of the cup of suffering which the Father had set before Him.

Almost six hours had passed since the nails were driven through His hands and feet. The worst was over. The tortures of hell had been endured in those horrible hours when His

Father had forsaken Him. Now He had again begun to see the friendly face of the Father who loved Him. We read, "After this, Jesus knowing that all things were now accomplished, that the scripture might be fulfilled, saith, I thirst."

He said this, that the Scripture might be fulfilled. The Old Testament prophecies were the frames into which the pictures of the New Testament fulfillment had to be fitted. Here one more fulfillment was placed in its proper fitting, a word from the Sixty-ninth Psalm. Centuries before, the sweet singer of Israel, David, had envisioned this Good Friday scene, and had written, "They gave me also gall for my meat; and in my thirst they gave me vinegar to drink."

It was not, however, primarily to fulfill prophecy that He cried out, "I thirst." Now, when all was accomplished, now when He was no longer forsaken of God, now when His soul-suffering was ended, now His tortured body cried out for attention.

Of all privations, heat and cold, aches and sores, wounds and bruises, nothing causes greater anguish than thirst. The feverish patient, the wounded warrior, the marooned sailor — their greatest need is water. When the rich man in hell lifted up his eyes, he pleaded that Lazarus dip his finger in water and cool his burning tongue. "I thirst!" This was the outcry of great bodily anguish. Exposed to the elements for six long hours, blood seeping from His pierced hands and feet, His throat parched, His tongue cleaving to the roof of His mouth; no wonder that He cried out, "I thirst."

No tongue will ever tell what He endured for our sakes, as our substitute, to atone for our sins. Here is the mighty God, who "maketh the clouds his chariot," who moistens the earth that it may bear fruit, who fills the fountains of the deep, pleading for a drop of water. And instead they gave Him vinegar.

As we hear the Saviour cry out in His thirst, there are two things we must not overlook. He, the mighty God, is also a true man. He is our flesh and blood. He took our human nature upon Himself. Only thus could He become our Redeemer, by exposing Himself to all the temptations which beset us, by suffering all the horrors and tortures to which we are subject, because we sinned. The agonies of thirst which He suffered upon the cross were, therefore, an intergral part of His work of redemption.

The torture of a human being, dying from thirst, is beyond description. The man lost in a desert, staggering along under the burning sun, futilely chasing a mirage, finally falling to the ground from utter exhaustion, as he sees the vultures hovering overhead, is indeed a picture of complete misery. But even that only dimly portrays the tortures that awaited us in damnation. From that He saved us. He thirsted so that He might give us that living water of which He spoke to the Samaritan woman at Jacob's well. He thirsted so that He might extend to us the invitation penned by Isaiah centuries before, "Ho, everyone that thirsteth, come ye to the waters, and he that hath no money; come ye, buy, and eat; yea, come, buy wine and milk without money and without price."

Such love must beget love. When we weigh all He suffered for us against what He asks of us, our hearts must melt within us. All He asks of us is that we by faith accept the sacrifice which He made for us, and that we love Him. Can we do less? God forbid! *Amen.*

# 16

## *"It Is Finished." Your Salvation Is Finished*

### (The Sixth Word)
### John 19:30

*When Jesus therefore had received the vinegar, he said, It is finished: and he bowed his head, and gave up the ghost.*

God's work of creation was finished on a Friday. Of that first Friday we read, "Thus the heavens and the earth were finished." On that first Friday it was God the Father who said, "It is finished." The creation of the world was finished. When the recreation of the sinful world was finished on Good Friday, it was God the Son who cried out, "It is finished."

This triumphant word of our Saviour turned the worst of all Fridays into Good Friday. It transformed the cross from an instrument of shame into a symbol of glory.

"It is finished." These words shook the earth. "The earth quaked and the rocks were rent." But these words also shook hell, and they shook heaven. At their sound Satan gnashed his teeth in helpless fury. He had exhausted all his ingenuity in his determination to prevent the Saviour from finishing the work of redemption. Soon after the incarnation of our Lord he had instigated Herod to murder the babes of Bethlehem, hoping that the Christ-child would be among them. At the beginning of the Saviour's ministry he had approached him with his threefold temptation. At the end he entered the heart of Peter, who sought to persuade his Master not to go to Jerusalem to suffer and to die. He had prompted Judas to betray Him. He had aroused the hatred of the leaders who plotted the death of their Messiah. And now he received that crushing blow, which recalled to his mind the threat which God had voiced in Paradise. "It is finished." For Satan these words stripped him of his power.

"It is finished," He announced to the prophets of the Old Testament. When three days later He opened the eyes of the two disciples on their way to Emmaus, it was but to show them how all the words spoken by the prophets were fulfilled. He opened their eyes to see what David foretold when he said, "My own familiar friend, in whom I trusted, which did eat of my bread, hath lifted up his heel against me." They had seen Judas do that. Now they understood what Zechariah meant when he wrote, "So they weighed for my price thirty pieces of silver." Now they had witnessed the fulfillment of Isaiah's prophecy, "I gave my back to the smiters, and my cheeks to them that plucked off the hair; I hid not my face from shame and spitting." As Psalm 22 had announced, they had heard Him cry out, "My God, my God, why hast thou forsaken me?" And as the same psalm had foretold, the soldiers had parted His garments among them, and had cast lots upon His vesture. Now all the prophets had their reward; to all He said, "It is finished!"

"It is finished," He said to His Father. "Thy will has been done. I have finished the work which thou gavest me to do. I have been obedient, even unto my death upon the cross."

"It is finished." Above all, these words are addressed to you. Do you know what these words mean for you? They mean just what they say. Your redemption, your salvation is finished. The utmost possible has been done, completed to the minutest detail Nothing remains to be added. Christ took upon Himself the sins of the world, your sins and mine, and He suffered their penalty. He died as your substitute. And God is just. He cannot punish the same offense twice. Since Christ justified you, you are no longer guilty. The Apostle says, "We thus judge, that if one died for all, then were all dead." "It is finished." That is Christ's solemn word given to you from the cross, assuring you that you are now the redeemed and forgiven child of God.

"It is finished." Immediately comes divided corroboration; the sun shines forth through the darkness which had settled on all the land. The curtain in the temple is torn from top to bottom, a heavenly invitation to come directly to the throne of grace without further sacrifice or priestly intervention. All nature joins to echo and re-echo the shout of the conqueror, "It is finished!"

No more glorious words have been spoken. May the Holy Spirit fully open your eyes to see their significance. What is finished is finished. Nothing can be stated more emphatically. What a pity that men still prattle of sacrifices for the atonement of sin, when the Word of God so clearly says, "Now where remission of these is, there is no more offering for sin." What could be clearer than the words, "For by one offering he hath perfected forever them that are sanctified."

Thank God for the comfort of the word, "It is finished." He that believeth that word shall be saved. "This is most certainly true." *Amen.*

# 17

## The Father's Hands —
## the One Safe Place for Your Spirit

### (The Seventh Word)
### Luke 23:46

*And when Jesus had cried with a loud voice, he said, Father, into thy hands I commend my spirit: and having said thus, he gave up the ghost.*

Two thousand years before our Lord's death Abraham was pleading with God to spare Sodom. As God lent a favorable ear to his prayer, he ventured ever more boldly to draw on divine patience and mercy. He said, "I will speak yet but this once."

Here on the cross hung He of whom the people said, "Never man spake as this man speaks." And now He was saying, "I will speak yet but this once." As children stand around a dear father's deathbed and strain their ears to hear his final words, so we now should be all attention to hear our Saviour's final words from the cross.

Under the cross stood the Roman centurion who had been commissioned to execute the death sentence which Pilate had pronounced. No sooner had the echo of the Saviour's last words been stilled when this centurion cried out, "Surely this was a righteous man, and the Son of God."

What was it that wrenched this confession out of the heart of this Roman? The last words of our Lord. Not only their meaning, not only their force, but the manner in which they were spoken, and the circumstances under which they were spoken, and their immediate result.

Almost always the dying surrender their souls with a barely audible sigh. There is no longer strength to speak or cry out. The pulse grows weaker and weaker, the heartbeat ceases. This was always true of those who died by crucifixion. Death was not primarily caused by loss of blood; for of that there was only a trickle. It was utter exhaustion which, after hours of unspeakable torture, finally took its toll. Speech was impossible because the parched tongue could no longer form words. In the case of the two thieves, the mockery of the one and the prayer of the other had ceased. They were beyond the power of speech when the soldiers broke their bones.

The death of Christ was altogether different. He cried with a loud voice. Exhaustion had not claimed Him, pain had not slain Him. Even now He could have postponed death, or escaped it. He died when He was ready to die because He wanted to die. Now He proved His word, "I have power to lay down my life, and I have power to take it again." Now He was ready to lay down His life, and by His own power over life and death, He laid it down. The two malefactors had to wait till death was ready to come, but He compelled death to come when He was ready.

"Father, into thy hands I commend my spirit." Literally translated, the words read, "Father, I deposit my soul into thy keeping." And this He cried with a loud voice. "Father, now I deposit my soul into thy keeping," and immediately He bowed His head in death. The centurion was shaken to the very depth of his heart. He knew that he had just seen the greatest miracle of his life. He knew that Jesus did what no human being could have done. He had commanded death to come to Him, and death had obeyed the command.

Since the Fall every man has not only been liable to death, but has deserved it; as all have forfeited their lives because of sin. Jesus, having never sinned, had not forfeited His life. He, alone, did not have to die; He died because He laid down His life as a sacrifice for the sin of the world. He had the power to terminate His life when the sacrifice was fully made. This the centurion now understood.

It was only to be expected that the Saviour would die with a word of Holy Writ on His lips. The nearer He came to the hour of death the more He pointed to the Scriptures and their prophecies. "The scriptures cannot be broken," He said. "The scriptures must be fulfilled." No sooner was He risen from the dead than He opened the Scriptures to two of His disciples, as He walked with them along the way. With a word of Scripture on His lips, He died. For in the Thirty-first Psalm we find these words, "Into thy hand I commit my spirit." May we, too, so live in the Scriptures that death may find us with a Word of God on our lips.

We may not speak these words in the exact sense in which Jesus spoke them, since we lack the power to lay down our lives at our pleasure. But because He spoke these words as our substitute, we can now repeat them in the sense that we are ready to deposit our souls in God's hands when He calls us. Thus St. Stephen in his final moments prayed, "Lord Jesus, receive my soul." Elijah, moaning under the juniper tree, cried out, "It is enough; now O Lord, take away my life." Thus Jonah prayed, "Take, O Lord, I beseech thee my life from me."

"Father into thy hands I commit my spirit," these were the last words of Polycarp, of Huss, of Melanchthon, and of Luther. May these words constitute our final prayer. The Saviour earned for us the right so to pray. *Amen.*

# 18

## Listen! Christ Is Speaking to You From the Upper Room

### (Maundy Thursday)
### Luke 22:19

*And he took bread, and gave thanks, and brake it, and gave unto them, saying, This is my body which is given for you: this do in remembrance of me.*

Ever since the day when Adam for the first time saw his own face, perhaps mirrored in some crystal-clear pool in Paradise, every man has stood face to face with himself, beholding himself and appraising himself. In such a moment of self-perception David exclaimed, "I will praise thee; for I am fearfully and wonderfully made."

One of the wonders of God's creative workmanship is man's memory. Nothing adds more to the enjoyment of life than the faculty to remember past impressions and events. Without a memory we would lead a very drab existence. Not that memories are always pleasant. Robert Cameron Rogers says, "O memories that bless and burn." Nevertheless it is far better to have the memories which burn together with those that bless, than not to have memories at all.

Who would journey afar to see the Grand Canyon, or the

Swiss Alps, or enchanting islands of the sea, if he could not retain in memory a picture of such scenes? Memory is our diary with which we relive the red-letter days of our past.

Memory is so vital to our well-being that, beginning with childhood, we resort to all sorts of tricks to make it tick. When the child recites, "Thirty days has September, April, June, and November," it is merely filing away data in the cabinet of memory. The victim of amnesia suffers sadly from loss of memory. To sit in endless brooding only to have the past keep eluding capture by the mind means unspeakable anguish.

Memory must always be one of the Christian's most prized possessions. Without it there could be no growth in Christian knowledge, and no advance in holiness of life. The remembrance of God's goodness and mercy in the past, coupled with memory of our own successes and failures, is a powerful aid to our spiritual development. No wonder that the Bible so often appeals to our memory. Moses admonished the children of Israel, "Remember this day in which ye came out of Egypt." The psalmist says, "They shall abundantly utter the memory of thy great goodness, and shall sing of thy righteousness." We are told, "Remember Lot's wife." Who knows whether Peter would have repented of his denial if he had not "remembered the words of Jesus." When David prayed, "Lord, remember not the sins of my youth," it was but the confession that he remembered them, and repented.

Yes, our memory alone compels us to join in the grateful acknowledgement of David, "I will praise thee; for I am fearfully and wonderfully made."

And with man's desire to remember goes his heartfelt wish to be remembered. Countless memoirs and autobiographies have been written by men eager to perpetuate themselves in the minds of men. Monuments and tombstones are efforts in the same direction. Absalom erected his own monument before his tragic death, saying, "I have no son to keep my name in remembrance."

On this Maundy Thursday evening there comes to us the touching appeal of our Saviour, uttered only a few hours before His death, "This do in remembrance of me."

Did our Saviour fear that He would be forgotten? There are more memorials to Him than to all the heroes of the world put together. Not merely books, but libraries, have been written concerning Him, concerning His work, His aims, His life, and His influence. The world's greatest artists produced their greatest masterpieces in their striving to express their conception of His likeness — Leonardo da Vinci's "Last Supper," Hofman's "Christ in Gethsemane." The sculptors wielded their chisels, and forth came "Thorwaldsen's Statue of Christ," the huge Christ of the Andes between Argentina and Chili. The silversmiths and goldsmiths fashioned their crosses and crowns, and poets sang their sweetest songs to Him. Wherever Christians have buried their dead they carved in marble and granite the confession of their faith in Him, who is the "Resurrection and the Life."

However, not to the painters and sculptors, writers and poets did Christ make His plea to be remembered, but to the Christian heart.

Christ was and is true man, human in every respect, save that He, alone, was without sin. His nature was like unto our nature, differing from us only in this that He was perfect and holy. In Him dwelt all the natural longings of our nature. He longed for understanding, sympathy and love, even as we do. In the Garden of Gethsemane His very heart cried out for sympathy when He said, "What, could ye not watch with me one hour?" His heavenly Father heard that cry. When men denied the suffering Saviour their sympathy, the Father sent an angel to strengthen Him. As He yearned for sympathy, so He also desired to be remembered by His disciples and friends; for the wish to be remembered is as human as the longing for sympathy. Nevertheless, when He said, "This do in remembrance of me," He was not voicing a human longing to be remembered. Not for His own sake, but for the sake of His disciples, and for our sake, did He ask to be remembered.

The last official Passover had just been celebrated, now came the first celebration of the new covenant, the Lord's Supper. At the Passover the Jews sang the "hallel," a song composed of portions selected from some of the psalms. The songs of the Exodus from Egypt, the separation of the Red

Sea, the law-giving on Sinai, the resurrection of the dead, and the suffering of the Messiah, were among these events perpetuated in their Passover Hymn, not for the sake of the events, but for the sake of the people, to remind them of God's goodness in the past and to remind them of their coming Redeemer.

When the Saviour said, "This do in remembrance of me," He gave His disciples a new "hallel" for the old Passover hymn. For their own sake, for the sake of their soul's salvation, they were to remember His atoning suffering and death. Whenever He appealed to the memories of His disciples, He did so for their own benefit. No sooner was He risen from the dead when the angel appealed to their memories, saying to the women who had come to His grave, "Tell his disciples and Peter that he goeth before you into Galilee; there shall ye see him, as he said unto you." They were to remember His promise, and take comfort. The time came when there was joy, comfort, and strength for the disciples in every remembrance of Him. Even Pentecost had not completely set Peter free from old inhibitions and prejudices. It required a vision, the cloth let down from heaven, filled with foods Peter had never tasted under Old Testament restriction, before he was ready to preach in the house of the Gentile, Cornelius. However, after He had preached there and had seen the Holy Spirit poured out upon those to whom He had proclaimed the Gospel, he joyfully admitted, "Then remembered I the word of the Lord, how he said, John indeed baptized with water; but ye shall be baptized with the Holy Ghost." When suffering, persecution, and death faced the disciples there was always the precious remembrance of His words and promises to give them confidence, courage, and strength. Again and again Peter, James, and John relived that day of days when He was transfigured before them on the mount, when they saw Him in His heavenly glory. Years later, Peter wrote in his epistle, "This voice which came from heaven we heard, when we were with him in the holy mount."

This evening He stands before us, as He once stood before His disciples, and says, "This do in remembrance of me." This do, not for my sake, but for your sakes.

Four thousand years before, a mighty war had begun, when Satan led our first parents into sin. The decisive battle of that war was now to be fought. On this eve of the battle Satan was marshaling all his forces. Judas had already signed the nefarious contract to betray Him; Caiaphas was drumming up a meeting of the Sanhedrin in anticipation of His capture; the soldiers and guards stood ready to follow the traitor wherever he should lead them. Had the Saviour been completely unaware of all this, He could not have proceeded with greater calmness and deliberation. In fact, He was already celebrating the victory. He was ordaining a Sacrament for the Church which was to grow out of His suffering, death, and resurrection. For Him, His death for the sins of the world was already an accomplished fact. No sooner was the last Passover Supper ended when the celebration of the Lord's Supper began. The Passover has served the believers of the Old Testament as a reminder of God's promise to send the Messiah. The Lord's Supper was to serve the New Testament believers as pledge and seal that He did come, and that He did atone for sin.

God laid the sin of the world on His Son. When Jesus died, His was a substitutionary death because He died for the sin of the world. On the third day God raised Him from the dead and thereby solemnly declared that the sins of all men were forgiven. "He that believeth this and is baptized shall be saved." That includes us. But God did not rest there.

Whenever we become a part of a great audience, we are more conscious of the fact that the speaker is addressing many than we are of the fact that he is addressing us personally. We may even be under the impression that his words apply more to others than to us. And sometimes they do. Every speaker knows, the larger the audience the greater the danger of impersonalization. Fully cognizant of this, the Saviour not only ordained the Gospel in which He addresses all men, everywhere, but He also ordained the Lord's Supper in which He approaches the individual. In the Sacrament He does not speak to you as to one among many, but He takes you aside from all the rest, and says, "Given and shed for you, for the remission of your sins." Here, *you,* take and eat My body, given for *you*; here, *you,* take and drink My blood shed for you.

It is for your own sake that He wants you to remember Him, so that you may always be conscious of the eternal truth that by His suffering and death He redeemed you from your sins.

May the Holy Spirit strike a lively and responsive chord in your heart as often as you hear these words, "This do in remembrance of me." *Amen.*

# 19

## Christ, Smitten by God's Justice and Man's Injustice

### (Good Friday)
### Isaiah 53:8

*He was taken from prison and from judgment: and who shall declare his generation? for he was cut off out of the land of the living: for the transgression of my people was he stricken.*

Good Friday, while contrasting the love of God and the wickedness of man, portrays the one at its height and the other at its depth. The love of God is so boundless that He gives His only begotten Son into death to save sinners from damnation; and the depravity of man is so bottomless that the sinful creature does not shrink from laying violent hands on the Creator. Yes, this is the day of most striking contrasts; for, on the one hand, we marvel at the lofty regions to which the love of God can soar; and, on the other hand, we shudder at the fathomless depths to which human sinfulness can plunge.

Paradoxical as it may sound, the death of Christ is attributable to God's justice no less than to man's injustice. God is righteous. He must punish each and every sin. Anything else would be inconsistent with His holiness. Once Christ offered Himself as our substitute, taking our sins upon Himself, the Father had no choice; He had to inflict punishment to the fullest extent. And "the wages of sin is death." On the other hand, it is no less true that man by his unrighteousness caused the death of Christ.

In the Garden of Gethsemane Christ prayed, "My Father, if possible, remove this cup from me." There was no answer. There could be no answer. Both God's righteousness and man's unrighteousness were unrelenting, both insisting that He drink the bitter cup to its dregs. Every charge brought against Him only served to establish His innocence more clearly, but man's stubborn wickedness would not let Him be exonerated. And God dealt with Him as if He, and He alone, had committed every sin, because He had taken the sin of the world upon Himself.

There was, therefore, no one on Good Friday, Neither in heaven Nor on earth, to declare His innocence. To this the prophet makes reference in the text when he says, "He was taken from prison and from judgment; and who shall declare his generation?" "Who shall declare his generation?" means, "Who shall publish the manner of His life; who shall declare His innocence?"

From the Mishna and other ancient writings we learn of an old custom in Israel, which had become a law. When a man, having been convicted of a capital crime, was led to his punishment, a public crier went before him shouting the words, "Whosoever knows anything of this man's innocence, let him come and declare it." It was an effort extended to the very last moment to prevent the execution of an innocent man. Nothing of the kind was done in the case of Jesus. Centuries before, the prophet had asked, "Who will do that for the Messiah?" It seems that the Saviour made reference to this law during His trial when He answered the high priest Caiaphas, "I spake openly in the world; I ever taught in the synagogue, and in the temple, whither the Jews always resort; and in secret have I said nothing. Why askest thou me? ask them who heard me, what I have said unto them; behold, they know what I said." It was a challenge to Caiaphas to let proper witnesses speak.

Years later Paul referred to the same law and complained that it was ignored in his case also. He said, "My manner of life, from my youth, which was at the first among mine own nation at Jerusalem, know all the Jews, which knew me from the beginning, if they would testify...."

From the four Gospels we know that this law was ignored in the case of Jesus. In fact, His enemies hurried His execution before proper witnesses could appear. In prophetic vision Isaiah had foreseen this when he said, "Who shall declare his generation?" Who would come forth to speak of His good and holy life, and declare His innocence? There was no one. God's righteousness would not let Him do it, and man's wickedness would not let them do it.

There was no public crier to go before Him, shouting, "Whosoever knows anything of this man's innocence, let him come and declare it." There were none to declare His innocence, but many were loudly crying out false accusations against Him. Led by their fanatic leaders, a mob of people shouted mockery and insult to make Him appear the vilest of the vile.

The more we read the 53rd chapter of Isaiah the more we are puzzled to understand how Israel could reject its Messiah. Scribes, priests, and elders all knew their Bible. Thirty-three years before, when the wise men came to Jerusalem, and when Herod demanded they tell him where Christ should be born, the scribes and priests quickly furnished the answer; for they knew Micah's prophecy, which designated Bethlehem as His birthplace. From Daniel's prophecy they knew when He should be born. Hence, when John the Baptist arose, we read, "They were in expectation." They knew that the time had come for the Messiah to appear. They knew this 53rd chapter of Isaiah. When they saw Jesus keeping silent before Pilate and Herod, they must have been reminded of the words, "He is brought as a lamb to the slaughter, and as a sheep before her shearers is dumb, so he openeth not his mouth." They clearly saw His innocence, and their own wickedness was before them, they must have been smitten by their recollections of the words, "He was wounded for our transgressions, he was bruised for our iniquities." When they saw Him hanging between two criminals and later buried in the tomb of the rich Joseph of Arimathea, their consciences must have again been aroused, as they remembered the prophecy which foresaw this so vividly.

Think of the words which form the second part of the text, "He was cut off out of the land of the living; for the transgression of my people was he stricken." The responsible people of Israel knew that the entire 53rd chapter of Isaiah speaks of the Messiah. No doubt, they had never fully understood how and why the Messiah should be "cut off out of the land of the living," how and why He should die a violent death. Now they, themselves, had brought it about. It was not that they were blind to the possibility that He was the Messiah when they plotted His death. They knew His claims concerning Himself. That very morning they had informed Pilate that He called Himself the Son of God. And despite their bold aggression, they were very much afraid of Him; for no sooner was He dead than they ran to Pilate to beg for troops to watch the grave. They knew what they feared. He had told them that He would arise on the third day.

"For the transgression of my people was he stricken." For fifteen hundred years they had annually celebrated the Passover as a reminder that one day the Lamb of God should shed His blood for their sins. And they had either seen or heard how John had pointed to Him as the Lamb of God which would take away the sin of the world. And now it was done. For the sins of the people He had been stricken to death. They had heard His dying cry, "Father, into thy hands I commend my spirit." And to that God immediately added a mighty *Amen* when the earth quaked, and the rocks were rent, and graves were opened. I wonder whether Caiaphas was in the temple when the great veil was torn from top to bottom at the very moment of His death?

There is nothing more wonderful in the life of Christ than His death. "For the transgression of my people was he stricken." With a loud voice He had cried out, "Father, into thy hands I commend my spirit," and immediately He had bowed His head and died. The fact that He still had the strength to cry out with a loud voice, and yet could die a moment later, did not only shake the Roman centurion to the depth of his being, but like the blow of a hammer, it drove home the truth in the hearts of the people that His life had not been taken from Him, but rather that He had laid it down as a sacrifice for the sin of the world. And when the mighty signs in nature followed, the conscience-stricken people smote on their breasts and asked themselves, "What have we done?"

"What have we done?" That must be our Good Friday question also. But then, with awe, and wonder, and gratitude and love, in repentance and faith, we must ask, "What hath God done?" God gave His only begotten Son into death for our sins, so that we might be justified. For Him, as He walked to His death on that Good Friday, there was no one to go before Him and declare His innocence. We are most forunate. As we walk toward our graves, in the direction of what without Him would lead to eternal death, His blood goes before us crying out, "These are they which have come out of great tribulation, and have washed their garments white in the blood of the Lamb. Says the poet,

> *Abel's blood for vengeance*
> *Pleaded to the skies;*
> *But the blood of Jesus*
> *For our pardon cries.*
>
> *Lift we then our voices,*
> *Swell the mighty flood*
> *Louder still and louder*
> *Praise the precious blood.*
> *                    Amen.*

# 20

*Christ Is Risen! Why Weepest Thou?*

(Easter)
John 20:15

*Jesus saith unto her, Woman, why weepest thou? whom seekest thou? She, supposing him to be the gardener, saith unto him, Sir, if thou hast borne him hence, tell me where thou hast laid him, and I will take him away.*

If you have driven your car through the uninhabited, rain-less, barren regions of our West, where only scrawny cacti and other desert plants break the monotony and dreariness of the scene, then you will remember the sigh of relief which arose from within you when you reached a natural oasis or an irrigated section, where life-giving water clothed the desert with a green garment and where miles and miles of orchard trees were laden with luscious fruit.

What water can do for desert-lands, the resurrection of Christ did for the spiritually dry and barren human race. In his prophetic vision Isaiah saw the entire family of man as a fruitless waste, from which the Redeemer would spring as "a root out of dry ground." The unspeakably dry and fruitless human desert had now been irrigated by the all-atoning blood of the Lamb of God. It was a redeemed earth that was greeted by the rising sun of Easter morn. The resurrection of the Lord effected a mighty transformation. The variance in the meaning of the word Easter is symbolical of the incredible change brought about by the glorious resurrection of Jesus Christ.

Easter took its name from Eostre, and Anglo-Saxon goddess, whose festival was celebrated in the spring of the year. According to legend Eostre changed her pet bird into a rabbit, which despite outward appearance, still laid eggs. Hence our Easter bunny, who builds nests and fills them with colored eggs. Easter Sunday — Sunday was the day for the worship of the sun, as Monday was for the moon. Who thinks of that now? Everything has a new meaning. Easter is the Day of Resurrection. Sunday could now be spelled Sonday; for it is the special day of the Son of God.

"This is the day the Lord hath made!" This is the day of Christian joy. And we do not permit our joy to be lessened by the fact that today we see people in our house of worship who will not be seen again before another Easter. Rather we see their presence as an acknowledgment on their part that even the indifferent and careless ones cannot escape the consciousness that this day should have meaning for them also. Nor do we let our gladness be shrouded by the behavior of some, more interested in the "new look" than in the "new birth," to whom this is merely the day of the Easter parade. Even the deplorable situation in churches which approach the Gospel of Easter with indifference can't dampen our joy.

Sad to say, many who insist that they be numbered among Christians doubt the physical resurrection of Christ. They say, "It matters not that the historical Christ rests in His grave under the Judean stars. The imporant thing is that He was willing to die for His convictions, leaving us an example of steadfastness and faithfulness to ideals."

Only Easter gives certainty to us, and lends meaning to the entire life and work of Christ. Without Easter, Good Friday would merely have been a day of tragedy, and would have been forgotten long ago. He who does not go on from Golgotha with its cross to Joseph's garden with its empty tomb can have no true and saving faith. The empty cross is the symbol of our redemption, but the empty tomb is God's signature to the amnesty that was proclaimed when our Lord bowed His head in death. It is the final vindication of His claim that He is the Son of God; it is full proof that His Word is true; it is the final, convincing, and clinching evidence of our redemption; it is God's solemn declaration that the sins of all men are forgiven.

Christ Himself anticipated His resurrection as the undeniable corroboration of His every word and deed. When His authority was questioned by His enemies, He replied that He would put an end to their sneering questions by His resurrection, which would silence them completely. They had seen many of His miracles. They could not deny them. Frustrated, they told themselves, "If we let him thus alone, all men will believe on him." On one occasion, having just witnessed the healing of a man who was deaf and dumb, they had the temerity to ask Him for a sign, showing that He had authority to do these things. Their effrontery drew from Him a scathing reply: "A wicked and adulterous generation seeketh a sign and a sign shall not be given it except the sign of the prophet Jonas, for as Jonas was three days and three nights in the whale's belly so shall the Son of man be three days and three nights in the heart of the earth." Whenever Christ was asked for a sign which brooked no gainsaying or denying, He pointed to His resurrection from the dead. Were He not risen from the dead, there would be no celebrating today.

Nothing could be more in keeping with the spirit of Easter than our Lord's first spoken word after His resurrection. "Woman, why weepest thou?"

It seems a strange question. When we see a woman standing beside a newly made grave, we do not ask, "Why weepest thou?" We know why she is weeping, we know that a dear one has departed this life, and that her tears give vent to her sorrow. But the Saviour's question was quite in order.

Mary had failed to recognize Him. She had mistaken Him for the gardener. If Christ were not risen from the dead, the story would end here. Mary and a handful of others would have grieved over the loss of a friend for a time, and the world would soon have forgotten the entire affair.

However, the story did not end there. The Apostle says,

"But now is Christ risen from the dead." This changes everything. There was full reason for Christ's question, "Why weepest thou?" This was no time for weeping; this was the time for unconfined joy and gladness.

Men who would deny the physical resurrection of Christ realize, of course, that Christianity could not have established itself, and certainly could not have survived the bloody persecutions of the first three centuries, had not His disciples and followers been firmly convinced of His resurrection. "But," men say, "They believed the resurrection because they wanted to believe it, and were predetermined to believe it." Nothing could be farther from the truth. Mary did not believe it because she did not even give it a thought. She did not recognize Him because He stood before her in one form while she was looking for Him in another form. She was looking for a corpse, for a dead Christ, and, therefore, she did not recognize the living Christ.

This applied to the disciples also. The two who ran out to the grave, Peter and John, had not given the resurrection a thought. John, who wrote this Gospel, later made the shameful confession, "For as yet they knew not the scripture, that he must rise again from the dead." They should have known. Jesus had told them often enough; but because they could not understand that He should die, nor why He should die, they had not foreseen the need of a resurrection. The two disciples on the way to Emmaus did not recognize Him because they also thought of Him as a corpse.

In the great drama of our Lord's passion the scenes changed rapidly. There are three changes of scene on Maunday Thursday — the first is the upper room in Jerusalem, the second is the garden of Gethsemane, and the third is the palace of the high priest, Caiaphas. There were five changes of scene on Good Friday, — Pilate's judgment hall, Herod's palace, the way of sorrows, Golgotha, the place of execution, and finally, the cemetery in Joseph's garden.

For Easter morning the last scene is unchanged. Again it is the cemetery in Joseph's garden. But, oh! the cemetery looks so different. There are no soldiers watching the tomb; the great stone at its entrance is rolled away; there are no shadows of the night; angels, radiating heavenly glory, are present; the grave clothes in which His body had been wrapped, are cast aside; though unwound, they still show the measurements of the corpse they had contained. There was reason for the question, "Why weepest thou?" The time for weeping was over. He was risen from the dead.

It is altogether fitting that the joyous announcement of the resurrection was first made in a cemetery. Had sin not entered into the world, there would be no cemeteries. Burial grounds were mute witnesses of the power and of the triumph of sin. Men's bitterest tears had been shed at sepulchres. Here man's complete helplessness and utter hopelessness had found expression in weeping and wailing. All that was changed on Easter morning.

No longer need cemeteries express desolation and despair. Read the inscriptions on tombstones: "Asleep in Jesus"; "Here rests in peace"; "In Jesus' arms"; etc. Over this most ancient of battlefields there now resounds the cry of triumph, "For this corruptible must put on incorruption, and this mortal must put on immortality."

During the war, in the middle of the ocean, in the dark of the night, the Benares was struck by an enemy torpedo, and soon sank beneath the waves. Little Jack Keely, from the East Side of London, bound for the United States where he and other English children were promised food and all things children look for, was pulled into a rubber raft by three survivors. Immediately he asked, "Which way is America?"

Through Christ, risen from the dead, we can now have the same fortitude and determination. In the tempest of temptation, in the storms of life, in the throes of sickness and suffering, in the face of death, we can seek direction, and ask, "Which way is heaven?" And always, though darkness be ever so dense, we can see the light and hear the voice, "I am the way, the truth, and the life." "I am the resurrection and the life, he that believeth in me, though he were dead, yet shall he live. And he that liveth and believeth in me, shall never die."

You who grieve over your sins of the past — "Why weepest thou?" "He is the propitiation for our sins." You who have suffered pain and misfortune — "Why weepest thou?" "Neither death, nor life, nor angels, nor principalities, nor powers, nor things present, nor things to come, nor height, nor depth, nor any other creature, shall be able to separate us from the love of God, which is in Christ Jesus our Lord." You who mourn the death of a dear one — "Why weepest thou?" "Blessed are the dead which die in the Lord from henceforth." You who tremble at the thought of your own death — "Why weepest thou?" Listen, and you shall hear the assurance of Him who is the Truth, "Where I am, there shall my servant also be."

> *He lives to silence all my fears,*
> *He lives to wipe away my tears,*
> *He lives to calm my troubled heart,*
> *He lives all blessings to impart.*

Christ is risen! Hallelujah! *Amen.*

# 21

## *An Open Line to Heaven*

### (Ascension)
### Luke 6:12

*And it came to pass in those days, that he went out into a mountain to pray, and continued all night in prayer to God."*

The text selected has no direct bearing on the ascension of our Lord, which the Christian Church commemorates this day. Nevertheless, it serves our purpose admirably; for today our thoughts reach up into heaven, and our only means of communication with heaven is prayer. When our Lord, immediately after His baptism by His forerunner John the Baptist, knelt to pray, "the heaven was opened." Prayer is still the key which opens the door of heaven.

We can have insight into the life, mission, and work of our Redeemer only if we understand that in the years of His humiliation He did not always, nor fully, make use of His divine power and majesty, which were communicated to His human nature in His incarnation. Always His omnipotent power and His divine majesty were at His disposal. Though He was seen in the form of a servant — often weary and hungry and always overworked — He was, nevertheless, the almighty God, the Creator of all things.

Peter the Great, disturbed by the illiteracy, inefficiency, and barbarism of the Russian people, undertook the Herculean task of leading them to a better way of life. He realized, however, that he must first learn for himself what he hoped to teach his subjects. Stripping himself of his royal robes and of every show of might and power, he traveled incognito, visiting various countries of Europe. For two years he labored in shipyards, factories, fisheries, and on farms, finally appearing in London to observe Parliament and other branches of government. In his humiliating position he was, despite his outward appearance, the mightiest and most absolute monarch on earth. But, lest he fail in his purpose, he made no use of his power and lofty position.

That is precisely what Christ did in our behalf. Only by refraining from using fully His power and majesty could He achieve His purpose and become our Redeemer. He came to fulfill the law for us. He, the law-giver, could do this only by placing Himself under the law and becoming obedient to the law. "Ye shall be holy, for the Lord your God is holy." There was no holiness in us. He came to lead a substitutionary life of perfect holiness in our stead, which was possible only if He became one of us, if He lived our life, sharing our experiences and temptations. It would have been utterly ridiculous for Satan to approach Christ with his threefold temptation, if Christ had used His omnipotent power to withstand him, nor would such a victory over Satan have benefited us. No, Christ stood before Satan with no greater power of resistance than Adam possessed when he was tempted in Paradise. Had Christ made use of His power and majesty, He could not have become our substitute; He could not have shared our experiences, hungering, sleeping, suffering, dying, as we do. It was, therefore, only periodically and momentarily that He made use of His divine power; namely, when He performed His great miracles to help suffering mankind and to reveal Himself as the Son of God.

He prayed. Had He always and fully used His divine power and majesty, His prayers would have been senseless. There is nothing for which God must pray. Why should He pray when He has the power to fulfill His every wish? But, when He made no use of His power, when He lived as we do, subject to the same trials and temptations, He needed strength and guidance from His heavenly Father. He found it in prayer.

There is something very wonderful in this text. "And it came to pass in those days, that he went into a mountain to pray, and continued all night in prayer." His days were laden with a burden of work the equal of which no man has ever borne. There was time only for short prayers, more like a sigh than an utterance. Said the Evangelist on one occasion, "He sighed and looked up to heaven." Only by depriving Himself of sleep and rest could He find time to pray for the strength which He so sorely needed. On another occasion, so Mark tells us, "In the morning, rising up a great while before day, he went out, and departed into a solitary place, and there prayed." For Him prayer was not a perfunctory, routine habit, but a part of His life, growing out of His heartfelt need to communicate with His Father. His disciples had always prayed, but when they heard Him pray they realized that they were sheer novices, and pleaded with Him, "Lord, teach us to pray." They sensed that prayer was the very source and mainspring of His strength.

However, He did not pray for Himself only. When He spent entire nights in prayer, when He arose in the morning, long before break of day to pray: we may rest assured that He prayed for us also, even as He did in the upper room on Maundy Thursday evening. He came as our great High Priest. The two chief functions of the high priest throughout the Old Testament were to sacrifice for the people and to pray for the people. Christ, Our High Priest, whom all other high priests had merely foreshadowed, sacrificed Himself for us. That sacrifice, being the perfect sacrifice, and the all-atoning sacrifice, made an end of all sacrifices for sin. The Bible clearly states, "where remission of sin is, there is no more offering for sin." All sin offerings hereafter are sham and hypocrisy, belittling His perfect sacrifice. At best, they are the result of a woeful ignorance of the fact that the Father accepted the sacrifice of His Son as a full and perfect atonement for the sins of all the world. He no longer sacrifices, and there is no need for us to sacrifice for sin. On the other hand, touching the second of His high priestly functions, He still prays.

When Christ ascended into heaven, He did not shed His human nature. He is still the God-man. He still wears the scars of His hands, feet, and side, as His court jewels. He is still our flesh and blood. It is our brother, who sits at the right hand of God the Father.

If our brother were the ruler of the nation, or a man of great wealth and power, it would give us a feeling of security. We would rejoice to have a brother in position to help us in an hour of need and to do great things for us. Now, at the right hand of God we have a brother, a brother of whom it is said that "He sticketh closer than a brother." Could we ask for greater security? To make the outlook still brighter for all who believe on Him, the Bible assures us that "He ever liveth to make intercession for them."

Yes, He still prays. He prays for us, and He will continue to pray for us until the dawn of our ascension day. We have a direct line to heaven on which we can call Him by day or night, in storm and stress, in good days and evil days.

Surely, we should never let a day go by without lifting our eyes to heaven, to the throne of our Brother. In the days of the great immigrations it often happened that one member of a family came to America, promising to send for the others as soon as he could earn the passage money and prepare a place for them. How eagerly they awaited the day. Any information on their promised home, any news from America, was joyfully received. And so we are waiting to emigrate to a better country, where our Brother has gone before us to prepare a place for us. We know His address; we have an open line of communication. Let us make use of it.

When you lift your eyes to the skies to see your Brother, as He is worshipped by saints and angels, you do not only see Him, you see yourself. You see the contrast. It makes you humble and ashamed. You realize how unfit you are of yourself, without the cleansing influence of the Holy Spirit, to take your place before His throne. You feel uncomfortable, knowing that "all your righteousnesses are as filthy rags."

And from your troubled heart arises the prayer, "Make me more like Jesus."

Prayer must not only mean petition and thanksgiving, but also fellowship. Through prayer we live in God, and God in us. On Ascension Day the angels instructed the disciples not to depart from Jerusalem before the Holy Spirit should be outpoured upon them. Standing with the disciples, as we watch our Lord ascend into His home and our future home, let us also look forward to Pentecost, and pray, "Come, Holy Spirit, come. Come to lead us in all truth and to keep us in faith, come and teach us to pray, come to live in us, and to transform us, and make us ready to occupy the place which Jesus, our ascended Lord, has prepared for us." *Amen.*

# 22

## *The World Needs Another Pentecost*

### (Pentecost)
### Acts 2:1-13

*And when the day of Pentecost was fully come, they were all with one accord in one place. And suddenly there came a sound from heaven as of a rushing mighty wind, and it filled all the house where they were sitting. And there appeared unto them cloven tongues like as of fire, and it sat upon each of them. And they were all filled with the Holy Ghost, and began to speak with other tongues, as the Spirit gave them utterance. And there were dwelling at Jerusalem Jews, devout men, out of every nation under heaven. Now when this was noised abroad, the multitude came together, and were confounded, because that every man heard them speak in his own language. And they were all amazed and marvelled, saying one to another, Behold, are not all these which speak Galileans? And how hear we every man in our own tongue, wherein we were born? Parthians, and Medes, and Elamites, and the dwellers in Mesopotamia, and in Judea, and Cappadocia, in Pontus, and Asia. Phrygia, and Pamphylia, in Egypt, and in the parts of Libya about Cyrene, and strangers of Rome, Jews and proselytes, Cretes and Arabians, we do hear them speak in our tongues the wonderful works of God. And*

*they were all amazed, and were in doubt, saying one to an-
other, What meaneth this? Others mocking said, These men
are full of new wine.*

Since the days of childhood we have been thrilled by the
reading of the Whitsuntide Epistle. "Parthians, and
Medes, and Elamites, and the dwellers in Mesopotamia, and
in Judea, and Cappadocia, in Pontus, and Asia, Phrygia, and
Pamphylia, in Egypt, in the parts of Libya about Syrene, and
strangers of Rome, Jews and proselytes, Cretes and Arabians."
That was 1900 years ago. That was an internationalism of
the highest order and an ecumenicalism without precedent. It
was the dawn of the hope that Babel's curse might be removed from mankind. It was the birthday of the universal
Church of Jesus Christ, the founding of a world-confederation
of many tongues, nations, and races, which has outlived the
centuries, and which will not cease to exist until time is no
more.

Today nations, united in name, but disunited in reality, sit
in council in a structure of beauty, which has taken its place
among the skyscrapers of New York. Americans, Russians,
English, French, Chinese, Japanese, Belgians, Poles, Czecho-
slovakians, Germans, Finns, Italians, Swedes, Danes, and Nor-
wegians: all the world is represented as it once was in Jerusalem, on the day of Pentecost. There is an outward veneer of
peace and harmony, which, however, only serves to gloss over
the suspicions, distrusts, and hatreds underneath. The hope
for a lasting peace from that bickering assembly is so dim that
even Christians tilt to the side of inconsistency.

We assemble in our churches on Sundays and call upon
God to grant harmony, peace, and friendship to the nations
of the world; and then, outside on the sidewalks, we assure
each other it will never come to pass. What kind of prayer,
and what kind of faith in prayer is that? What are we doing?
What are we saying? In effect we are saying, "Heavenly Father, we are willing for You to have a try at it, but we doubt
that You can do anything about it."

Our weak faith, which lets us doubt God's ability to grant
what we ask, also inclines us to fold our arms in idleness, and

to say, "At any rate, there is nothing we can do about it." But are our hands really tied? Do we utterly lack the means of doing something for an improved relationship among men? Let us examine the facts.

First of all, let it be said that the Church, as such, has nothing to do with any peace conference aiming at the settlement of international disputes. Christ renounced any claim to a seat in such a conference for Himself, as well as for His Church, when He said, "My kingdom is not of this world." Nevertheless, churchmen lacking understanding of the fact that separation of Church and state is a divine ordinance, insist that the Church be heard. The pope, to whom separation of Church and state is anathema, has again and again offered his services. But Christ, who refused to act as a judge between two brothers at variance with each other in an inheritance matter, will not lend Himself as an arbiter between disputing nations. This does not mean, however, that the Church is not concerned about international disagreements, nor disinterested in peace among nations. She is vitally interested and earnestly prays for peace. Nor does it mean that we, as Christians, have no responsibility. We have the greatest responsibility. Our baptismal vow pledges us to war against Satan and all his work. War, and its hates and brutalities, are Satan's work. But we do not fight with carnal weapons.

Wherein then does our strength lie? To whom can we look for improvement in human relationships? Certainly not to the conclaves of the rulers of the nations, nor to their abortive peace treaties. A thousand peace conferences, and the treaties growing out of them, have resulted in dismal failure. More than 400 years ago Luther said, "Treaties have generally resulted in this that those from whom the greatest benefits were expected did the greatest harm." Always nations have been more interested in the division of spoils than in a lasting peace. When, at the end of World War I, Woodrow Wilson gave expression to lofty ideals at the peace conference, Clemenceau disdainfully said, "That man speaks like Jesus Christ." He preferred to speak the language of Nero, and of Attila the Hun.

What we Christians can do and should do is to apply the

lessons of Pentecost. Pentecost clearly demonstrated that salvation in Christ Jesus must be applied to the individual soul through the preaching of the Gospel." When Christ said, "Baptize all nations," He instructed His Church to baptize every individual in every nation. And when He said, "Preach the Gospel to all nations," He likewise implied that salvation must be applied to the individual soul through the preaching of the Gospel. Nations are baptized when the individuals in the nation are baptized, and nations are converted when their citizens individually are converted. Bringing Christ to the nation can only mean bringing Christ to the individuals in the nation. When the majority of any nation are truly brought under the influence and sway of the Gospel of Christ, the Prince of Peace, that nation no longer lets hate, and greed, and lust of power, and pride dominate its relationships with other nations, but it manifests tolerance, understanding, and sympathy. That is only logical and consistent. For the Christian knows that Christ shed His blood and died for men of all nations and races, even as He died for him. Christ drew no national or racial boundaries when He said, "A new commandment I give you, that ye love one another." The more Christians there are in a nation, the greater will be the desire to live at peace with other nations; and so the danger of war is lessened.

This process, however, seems too slow to many. They look for an individual or for a new system to superimpose its idealism upon the world, either by persuasion or by force. Others advocate that aggressors and evildoers at the head of the nation be eliminated, by fair means or foul, hoping that thereby aggression and evildoing will be eliminated from the nation itself. Even Christians sometimes feel that to convert a nation by converting its people one by one means too slow a pace. But that is Christ's way. When Christ enters a nation with His Word and Sacraments, He does not come to change the form of government, but to transform the hearts of the citizens. Far from demanding external changes, He calls unto all, "Let every man abide in the same calling wherein he was called." Quietly and unseen of men, Christ conquers entire commonwealths, but He leaves the king upon his throne, the statesman in his office, the judge upon his bench, the country its laws, the republic its liberty, and the cities their characters. Wherever He thus conquers, there new national ideals and new ways of life will soon be seen.

On Pentecost Day many nations were represented in Jerusalem, represented, however, by only a few individuals from any nation. But, as a little leaven leavens the whole lump, each little group became an influence in its respective nation. Soon were there not only thousands of Christians in the countries to which they returned, but undreamed of social reforms were established. When Paul went to Macedonia, he went to bring Christ to that nation; but he began with a few women at the bank of a river, and with a jailor in the vestibule of the city jail. No beginning was too humble for the great Paul. The conversion of a single soul was a triumph, and the signal for thanksgiving. The only way to help the world is by evangelizing and Christianizing the world. No matter how small or how slow the beginning, it is the only way; it is Christ's way. "Great oaks out of little acorns grow." That is always true in Christ's kingdom.

However, before we can do much in the great effort to evangelize the world, something must be done for us and to us; something akin to what happened to the disciples on Pentecost must happen to us also. They received "power from on high." By evening of that day they were different men. The same contrast between before and after in the life of Paul was first seen in them. There was a new tone. Even the enemies were aware of it. "They took knowledge of them that they had been with Jesus." Not only had they been with Jesus, but Jesus was still with them. They had received the Holy Spirit a great while before Pentecost. They were believers, and "no man calleth Jesus Lord, but by the Holy Ghost." As a result they had already done something for Christ, and for their fellowmen. No sooner had Andrew found Christ than he brought his brother, Simon. And Philip brought Nathanael. On two missionary journeys they had performed miracles. Now, however, they received a new and far greater measure of the Holy Spirit. The Holy Spirit was poured out on them. What great things they accomplished thereafter you know.

In Christ's kingdom a servant is utterly useless until he receives the Holy Spirit. When Paul reached Ephesus, he heard of Christians residing in the city. His first question was, "Have they received the Holy Spirit?" The success of any worker of Christ depends on the measure of the Holy Spirit which he has received. Of St. Stephen we read that "he was full of the Holy Ghost." In the Book of Acts there is the oft-repeated phrase, "they received the Holy Ghost," or, "and the Holy Ghost fell upon all that heard the word."

As for us: we received the Holy Ghost long ago; in our infancy, when we were baptized. He enlightened us, opening our eyes to the grace and mercy of our Lord Jesus Christ. Holding the mirror of God's holy law before us, He made us see ourselves as poor, lost, and condemned sinners. By the Gospel He enabled us to see and believe that Jesus died out of great love for us, and that in Him we have propitiation for all our sins. He engendered love in us for Him who first loved us. We have already accomplished something for the improvement of human relationships, inasmuch as we helped others to come to Christ, their Saviour.

However, what we have already done for Christ and for humanity is insignificant in comparison to what we could do if a thorough Pentecostal improvement would take place in us. And Pentecost gives us the assurance that it is possible, and that the heavenly Father stands ready to grant us an increased measure of the Holy Spirit if we desire it. That is what we need, and our weakness grows out of our failure to realize this fully.

If, before Pentecost, Jesus had established some petty Israeli Kingdom, and if He had appointed His disciples, the one as Prime Minister, the other as Secretary of State, and a third as Postmaster General, etc., they would have been completely satisfied. It would have been the gratification of their highest ambitions.

Sometimes we, likewise, are complacently satisfied with ourselves. We think of ourselves as the salt of the earth, ignorant of the fact that the salt has lost its savor. At such times we are like Peter, James, and John on the Mount of Transfiguration. Let the world go to smash, let mankind remain unredeemed. They liked the scenery and the company. How like ourselves! Where we are, and what we are is good enough. On Sundays we pray for the President and for Congress, and during the week we tell each other what incompetent and selfish people they are, and what we would do if our stations were reversed. The world is rotten because Christians, ourselves included, do so little to prevent rot. We sing, "Like a mighty army moves the Church of God," when in truth we resemble Coxey's Army. We cannot improve the world until there is improvement in us.

It can be done. How? Of those early Christians, who received the Holy Spirit in increased measure, we are told, "And they continued steadfastly in the apostles' doctrine and fellowship, and in the breaking of bread, and in prayers." That is the secret. Diligent use of the means of grace, and of prayer. There must be real fervency in your prayer, "Create in me a clean heart, O God, and renew a right spirit within me." There must be a heartfelt plea in your song, "Come Holy Spirit, God and Lord! Be all Thy graces now outpoured." The grip of Satan on the souls of men can be broken only by a power greater than our own. For that, we too need power from on high. The more we realize our own helplessness, and the more we pray for divine power, the more the balance of power will shift from the kingdom of Satan to the kingdom of Christ. May your Pentecost prayer then be that the Holy Spirit may make you a power in the war against the forces of darkness. He who hears prayer will hear your prayer. *Amen.*

# 23

## *The Trinity: Wisdom to Believers —*
## *Foolishness to Unbelievers*

### (Trinity Sunday)
### Romans 11:33-36

*O the depth of the riches both of the wisdom and knowledge of God! how unsearchable are his judgments, and his ways past finding out! For who hath known the mind of the Lord? or who hath been his counsellor? Or who hath first given to him, and it shall be recompensed unto him again? For of him, and through him, and to him, are all thingss to whom be glory for ever. Amen.*

From the first Sunday in Advent to Pentecost our hearts and minds have been occupied with a review of the great deeds of God for our salvation. Today our thoughts turn to the essence of God.

One thing all men have in common; they know there is a God. Only men bereft of all reason will deny the existence of a God. The Bible says, "The fool hath said in his heart, there is no God." All but fools know there is a God because conscience tells them so, and nature tells them so. "The heavens declare the glory of God; and the firmament showeth his handiwork."

All men agree that there is a God. There human knowledge stops. There men separate to walk on three different paths, each path having many by-paths. The polytheist, the monotheist, and the Trinitarian go their separate ways.

Who is the true God? Polytheism answers, "There are many gods, thousands of them — male and female, good and evil." Monotheism holds that there is but one God. Trinitarianism teaches that God is one in essence, but three in person. The heathen have their many gods; Mohammedans, Jews, Unitarians, and others insist that God is one in essence and in person; only Christians believe in a Triune God.

Left to themselves men never find the right answer. Human thinking and reasoning can never lead men to the knowledge of God. The Greeks boasted of their philosophies and of their learning. But the learned Greeks and the wise Romans knew no more of God than the dullest barbarians. If God had not given us the Bible, you and I would be worshipping idols. How could we ever unravel the mysteries of God? All around us are mysteries in nature, which we do not understand. The fact is, we are mysteries unto ourselves. We know little about our bodies, less about our minds, and still less about our souls. How could we know God, if God had not revealed Himself to us?

Even our language cannot encompass God. The Bible, itself, does not use the term "three persons." The paucity of our language compels us to speak of "persons." We have no words adequate to describe the Trinity.

The question is asked, "Why did not God tell us more of His Triune Being? Why did He not describe Himself in more explicit language?" What would be the use? The doctor of mathematics could describe calculus to his child, but he refrains because the child does not understand. Neither would we understand if God would more fully describe Himself to us. A tack-hammer is a proper tool for tacking, but not for driving home a railroad spike. The human mind is a proper instrument for the probing of many secrets, but not one to fathom the depths of God's being.

In His midnight conversation with Nicodemus the Saviour told him that there are heavenly truths which must be accepted by faith, because they cannot be comprehended by reason. And the Saviour furthermore told him that only by enlightenment of the Holy Spirit can we know God at all. God does not ask us to understand; He only asks of us to believe what He has revealed to us in His holy Word. The Saviour said, "If a man love me, he will keep my words; and my Father will love him, and we will come unto him, and make our abode with him." That is what our Saviour asks of us, a love that will take Him at His word and trust in Him. He, who revealed God to us, is the only way to God for us. He gives the lie to those who come with that hackneyed, shallow, Christ-denying platitude, which they utter so didactically, "We are all going to the same place by different roads." He said, "I am the way." Nothing could be more singular. Any other way leads to perdition. Make no mistake; anyone who attempts to shake your faith in the Triune God has a sinister purpose. He would rob you of your faith in Christ, your only Saviour.

If it were not so tragic, it would be ludicrous to hear the spiritual dunces, who are encountered daily, glibly voicing their opinions of God and of spiritual things, which are mysteries beyond comprehension of the greatest of Christian theologians. They feel nothing of the awe and wonder which gripped the heart of St. Paul when he said, "O the depth of the riches both of the wisdom and knowledge of God! how unsearchable are his judgments, and his ways past finding out!"

The discrepancy between the thinking of the humble child of God and the unenlightened unbelievers is never more apparent than when they speak of the justice and of the mercy of God. To the Christian the justice of God is far less mysterious than the mercy of God. The reverse is true of the unbeliever — to him the justice of God is a complete mystery, while he takes the mercy of God for granted.

Noah could understand why God would destroy a world which would not be led by the Spirit. He knew that divine justice had no alternative. While preaching repentance, he wielded the axe and the saw in the building of the ark, which would be his refuge when the anger of God should be unleashed. His unbelieving contemporaries, on the other hand, did not believe that God would destroy the earth because they saw no compelling reason for a display of stern justice. They went their wicked way until the flood engulfed them and silenced the curses on their lips.

The Christians of Jerusalem readily understood that Jerusalem was doomed because it had despised the Word of God, stoned the prophets, and crucified the Son of God. To the crucifiers the threat of the city's destruction sounded ridiculous and unreasonable. They refused to believe it. And when destruction came, they stood against the wall of wailing, and wept. They could not comprehend why God should visit so great an evil upon them, when they were Abraham's seed.

The thinking of believer and unbeliever undergoes no change through the ages. Their views of God's justice are poles apart. When a great calamity strikes some part of the world — war, pestilence, hurricane — the Christian sees God's answer to man's wickedness and rebellion. He humbly acknowledges that believer and unbeliever merit divine chastisement in the one case, and divine punishment in the other case. The unbeliever, on the other hand, accepts blame for nothing. He blames God. "How can God do such a thing?" "Why did God do this?" "Is this the merciful and loving God?" "God is not just." To the Christian, God's justice is comprehensible; to the unbeliever, it is always incomprehensible.

On the other hand, the child of God is always overwhelmed by the mercy of God, while the unbeliever takes it for granted. Thinking of his own sinfulness, of his own puny insignificance, as opposed to the holiness and majesty of God, the Christian can only join the Psalmist in his astonishment that God should be loving and merciful. He can only cry out, "What is man that thou art mindful of him? and the son of man, that thou visitest him?"

Why did God call Abraham from his obscure and distant home and settle him in Palestine, the corridor of the world, over which the armies and merchants of Egypt, Babylon, Nineveh, Assyria, Greece, and Rome marched back and forth, so that all the world could not but learn of the coming Messiah? Why did He raise up men like Isaac, Jacob, Moses, Elijah, Daniel, and David? What other little country ever produced such an array of greatness, not to speak of Isaiah,

Jeremiah, Gideon, Solomon, and others? The people stoned the prophets — God sent more prophets, with ever clearer revelations of the coming Messiah. Why? Pious prophets, priests, psalmists, judges, and kings could only speak in astonishment, awe, and wonder of God's mercy. They could not think of a single deed on their part, which merited it. They could only pray God to continue to be merciful, and not to enter into judgment with His servants.

The wicked in Israel took God's mercy for granted. Whether they knelt before the golden calf or before the idol Baal, whether they persecuted the prophets or turned God's house into a den of thieves — they expected God to be kind to them because they were Abraham's seed. That settled it.

And so it is now. The Christian understands God's justice, and can only marvel at His mercy; the unbeliever takes God's mercy for granted and curses God's justice. Why did God adopt you as His child in holy baptism? Why did the Holy Spirit in Sunday School, confirmation class, and church service enlighten you with His gifts? Why did He daily and richly forgive you all your sins? Why did He keep you in faith? For these and a hundred other questions you can find no answer. You can only say with Paul, "Of him, and through him, and to him, are all things: to whom be glory forever and ever."

"Who hath known the mind of the Lord?" Always God is a mystery to us, far, far beyond our comprehension. "We now see as through a glass, darkly." Be not disturbed. One day you shall see Him face to face. Meanwhile contine to ponder, and to wonder. Ask yourself again and again, "Who hath first given to him, and it shall be recompensed unto him again?"

Is God's mercy a recompense for anything we first gave Him? Perish the thought. We gave Him nothing to merit His mercy — He gave us everything. He gave us His Son, "and with him," says the Apostle, "he gave us everything." Yes, He gave us everything we need for time and eternity. He gave us body and soul; He gave us faith; He gave us the forgiveness of all our iniquities through the blood of His Son; He made us His children, and heirs of everlasting life. He did it all because He loved us, loved us so "that he gave his only-begotten Son, that whosoever believeth on him should not perish, but have everlasting life." And, so, again we say, "To whom be glory forever." *Amen.*

# 24

## *If You Come Short of Eternal Life, Do Not Blame Others*

### (Second Sunday After Trinity)
### II Peter 3:17

*Ye therefore, beloved, seeing ye know these things before, beware lest ye also, being led away with the error of the wicked, fall from your own stedfastness.*

When on Good Friday Pilate called for a basin of water and washed his hands before a great multitude, saying, "I am innocent of the blood of this just person," it was his refusal to accept responsibility for the death of the Just One, whom he had condemned to die, though, in the same breath, he had declared Him to be innocent.

The world is full of Pilates, who refuse to accept personal responsibility. In fact, if it were not for Christianity, the feeling of responsibility would be almost entirely foreign to man. Christians come by it through their understanding of the death of Christ. When the child of God sees his Saviour scourged, crowned with thorns, spit on, and crucified, he does not say, "The Jews did that"; "Pilate did that"; but he says, "I did that." He knows it was sin, also his own sin, that crucified the Lord. Out of his acceptance of responsibility for the death of Christ grows his sense of responsibility for other evils also.

Unbelievers are not thus conscious of their responsibility for existing evils. For them it is as natural as breathing always to blame others, while denying personal responsibility. This sin is as old as sin itself; for the first recorded word, which man spoke after the fall into sin, was a denial of responsibility. Adam said, in effect, "I am not responsible. The woman thou gavest me enticed me to eat." And Eve took up the refrain and said, "I am not responsible. The serpent beguiled me to eat." And their first-born son, murderer and liar, followed in their footsteps, when he said, "Am I my brother's keeper?"

Men shirk responsibility in national affairs, in civic affairs, in family affairs, and in personal affairs. When war comes, there is always a great avowal of self-righteousness coupled with a denial of responsibility. Incidents, not of our creation, are blamed; leaders of other nations are blamed; ideologies of other people are blamed. But that is merely paving the way for another war. The one and only cause of war is sin. We are all responsible because we are all sinners.

Daily, in a thousand conversations, officials of city, state, and federal government are blamed for evil and corruption. There will never be good government until citizens admit their personal responsibility. We vote for candidates after we decry their ineptness and dishonesty. That is hardly in keeping with the Word of God, which instructs us to "seek the peace of the city, and pray for it."

Our entire nation is at present perturbed by the prevalent juvenile delinquency. The root of it lies in the failure of parents to assume responsibility for the training of their own children. Recently, a judge in criminal court said to me, "I wish people knew how tired I grow of the everlasting repetition of the word jail, jail, jail. All the more because I know that in the majority of cases the jail term is punitive and not corrective. Only Christian homes, the Sunday School, and the Church can change this deplorable situation. We judges are helpless." But even the Sunday School and the Church are often helpless because parents do not cooperate by accepting their responsibility over against their children. The time to make a tree grow straight is when it is still a sapling.

Worse still is man's refusal to accept responsibility for his own faults and shortcomings. An oft repeated expression is, "I never had a chance. I never got a break." If it were left to the inmates of any prison, they would probably write, "Here are housed the unfortunates who never got a break" over the door of their detention home; when in reality every prison door could be inscribed with the words, "Here are housed the recalcitrants whose parents, or who themselves, refused to accept responsibility for their conduct."

Bad as the consequences are for those who shirk their responsibilities in ordinary life, even worse is the aftermath of this folly if pursued in their spiritual life. In the Gospel, which is read in our churches on this Sunday, we are told of a man who made a great supper, and invited many. The guests, spurning his invitation, and indifferent to his efforts in their behalf, offered the conventional excuses of people who fail to attend functions at which propriety and decency demand their presence. At the same time they refused to accept responsibility for their discourtesy. All blamed one thing or another for their failure to attend. But the host did not accept their excuses. "None of these," he said, "shall taste of my supper." In this Gospel our Saviour is speaking in parable. The great supper is our salvation, which God offers to us in Christ Jesus. All who refuse His gracious invitation are responsible for their own damnation. Their excuses are not accepted.

This is what the apostle has in mind when he says, "Beware, lest ye also, being led away with the error of the wicked, fall from your own steadfastness." Millions of professing Christians have fallen from their steadfastness. I am sure you have met many such. What did they have to say for themselves? Did even one of them ever say, "I have no excuse; I fell into the error of the wicked. It was my own fault. I listened to the voice of Satan, rather than to the voice of God." No one ever said that to me. Always it is the same story: their parents were too strict when they were young; or the Pastor said something which offended them; or there were too many hypocrites in the congregation. It was not their own fault. Others were to blame, others were responsible for their unsteadfastness.

However, the Apostle says, "Beware lest you fall from your own steadfastness." Backsliders always blame their downfall on the unsteadfastness of others. That is folly; for your salvation does not depend on the steadfastness of others, but on your own steadfastness. "Beware," says the apostle, "lest you fall from your steadfastness."

By the grace of God you became a Christian. Through baptism you were received into the communion of the Triune God. Through your spokesmen, your sponsors, you solemnly vowed to renounce the devil and all his evil works, and to serve the Triune God. For a time your steadfastness depended on your parents. They were in Christian duty bound to teach you, to take you to Sunday School and to Church, to send you to confirmation class. Thereafter, responsibility for your steadfastness shifted more and more from their shoulders to your own. Now your salvation depended on your own steadfastness. "Beware," says the Apostle, "lest you fall from your steadfastness." If you do, the responsibility is your own.

Can anyone who is not steadfast come before God, and say, "In my youth my parents were too strict"? Let us grant that there may be some truth in what you say. It is an admitted fact that some parents use poor judgment in the spiritual training of their children. No parent can be too strict in forbidding what is wrong. Nevertheless, there are parents who let their children taste too little of the sweetness and freedom of the Gospel and too much of the bitterness of the law. That stems from their own failure fully to see the glory of the Gospel. Think of the many parents, who have a warped view of the Sabbath, and forbid their children to engage in harmless play and recreation because they do not rightly understand that Christ, Himself, put an end to the Old Testament restrictions concerning the Sabbath. This may have been true in the case of some here present this morning.

Now you are matured; you stand on your own responsibility. Can any unfortunate experience in youth excuse you now, or justify you, if you neglect the word and the sacraments? Will God approve if you say, "My parents were not steadfast in clinging to the freedom of the Gospel; hence, neither am I steadfast?" I can only plead with you not to approach the judgment seat of God with an excuse so invalid. Your salvation does not depend on the steadfastness of others, but on your own.

Nothing is more important in your life than to break the habit of saying, "I am not responsible; I am not to blame." Learn to pray, "O God, show me where I am to blame, to the end that I can make amends and help others."

In the day of our Lord there was an accident in Jerusalem. Eighteen people were killed when the tower of Siloam collapsed and crushed them under its ruins. The Saviour commented on the accident and warned His hearers not to think the eighteen victims were sinners above all others in Jerusalem, but rather to repent, lest they likewise perish. It is far more important to look for flaws and faults in your own character, and to correct them, than to judge others.

Christ suffered and died to save us. He redeemed us, who were children of Satan, and made us children of God, and heirs of everlasting life. He can expect eternal gratitude. But, as we are by nature, steadfastness is not in us. Only the Holy Spirit, who brought us to faith, can keep us in faith. May we look to Him and may our constant prayer be,

*Lord do not let me waver, but give me steadfastness,*
*And for such grace forever, Thy holy name I'll bless.*
*Amen.*

# 25

## *The Holy Jesus Dealing with Vile Sinners*

### (Third Sunday After Trinity)
### Luke 15:1-10

*Then drew near unto him all the publicans and sinners for to hear him. And the Pharisees and scribes murmured, saying, This man receiveth sinners, and eateth with them. And he spake this parable unto them, saying, What man of you, having a hundred sheep, if he lose one of them, doth not leave the ninety and nine in the wilderness, and go after that which is lost, until he find it? And when he hath found it, he layeth it on his shoulders, rejoicing. And when he cometh home, he calleth together his friends and neighbors, saying unto them, Rejoice with me; for I have found my sheep which was lost. I say unto you, that likewise joy shall be in heaven over one sinner that repenteth, more than over ninety and nine just persons, which need no repentance. Either what woman having ten pieces of silver, if she lose one piece, doth not light a candle, and sweep the house, and seek diligently till she find it? And when she hath found it, she calleth her friends and her neighbours together, saying, Rejoice with me; for I have found the piece which I had lost. Likewise, I say unto you, there is joy in the presence of the angels of God over one sinner that repenteth.*

When the people, who heard Him, said of our Lord, "Never man spake as this man speaks," they marveled at the clarity, forcefulness, and authoritativeness of His words. No less were they impressed by His manner of speaking. As no other, He engaged their attention. He knew how people think, and, therefore, knew how to hold their thoughts.

"Then drew near unto him all the publicans and sinners for to hear him." They drew near to Him because He first drew near to them. Here we have a very forceful directive for our work in the Church. To gain people for Christ we must win them by kindness and avoid antagonizing them. In fact, this is an excellent rule for our conduct in every walk of life. Some Christians, seeking to gain others for Christ, devote time and effort uselessly because they antagonize people, and thereby only harden them in their resistance. They nag, they scold, they resort to sarcasm; and they reap resentment. Let us learn from our Lord to draw near to sinners, and to encourage them to become better; rather than to upbraid them for being bad.

It was a trying day in our Saviour's ministry. Look at the circumstances. On the one hand, there were around Him a great many publicans and sinners. Many were confirmed sinners who knew they were sinners. On the other hand, there were the self-righteous Pharisees, who did not admit that they were sinners; but their blatant hypocrisy stamped them as the most stubborn and the worst of sinners. Either class alone was bad enough; together they combined practically everything that was evil in the sight of God. Only the Saviour could deal tactfully and charitably with both; for He sought to help the Pharisees just as much as the publicans.

Here, at the same time, Jesus dealt with the highest and lowest strata of Jewish society — the Pharisees who considered themselves paragons of virtue and the elite among men, and the publicans and labelled sinners, the scum of society. Any ordinary minister of the Word might have said to the Pharisees, "Let me first rid myself of these other people, and then I will gladly meet with you." But the Lord saw only lost souls, all in need of salvation. In His eyes all were in the same class.

He addressed both groups simultaneously in three parables: the lost sheep, the lost coin, and the prodigal son. As we read them, we hardly know whether they were intended primarily to rebuke the Pharisees, or to comfort the publicans and sinners. He rebuked the former class, and He comforted the latter. The sins inherent in each group He exposed.

It began when the publicans and sinners drew near to hear Him, and when the scribes and Pharisees murmured, saying, "This man receiveth sinners and eateth with them."

The behavior of the Pharisees was not surprising. They were self-deluded creatures of self-righteousness, whose religion was a thing of outward morality and of political striving. On one occasion our Lord characterized them in His inimitable manner, when He said, "Woe unto you, scribes and Pharisees, hypocrites! for you make clean the outside of the cup and of the platter, but within they are full of extortion and excess. . . . ye are like unto whited sepulchres which indeed appear beautiful outward, but are within full of dead men's bones, and of all uncleanness."

With hearts filled with envy, hatred, and greed, they were, nevertheless, fastidiously exact in the observance of their own ceremonial regulations and laws. The mere touch of a publican or gentile, they thought, rendered them ceremonially unclean. Returning from the market, or some other public place, they washed themselves for fear that they might have inadvertently touched a gentile or sinful person. Yes, they also washed their pots and pans and furniture, which perchance might have been touched by a gentile or publican during their absence.

To them it was shocking that Jesus should receive publicans and sinners, and eat with them. In *Uncle Tom's Cabin,* Topsy said of Ophelia, her would-be reformer, "She would no more touch me than she would touch a toad." To the Pharisees all publicans and sinners were untouchables. Jesus, who came to befriend men and to save them, had to be in touch with them. I can imagine that a thrill must have run through the very being of the leper, whom Jesus touched. No doubt, he had not been touched by a human hand for a long time. Jesus never stood at a distance when He spoke and preached to publicans and sinners. They knew they were not welcome in decent society. The   publican in the temple stood afar off, and did not as much as lift up his eyes. That was not only the posture of a sinner in the presence of God, but it was also the behavior of one who was snubbed and avoided by his fellow men. For Jesus to help them, He first had to win their confidence and make them understand that they could come to Him with their problems without fear or embarrassment. To win them, He had to meet them on their own level, mingle with them, and eat with them.

There was no use in telling that to the Pharisees. They would not have understood. In their opinion, if Christ mingled with publicans and sinners, He was one of them, and no better than they. Their disdainful observation was, "Birds of a feather flock together." Since it was impossible to make them realize His own feelings concerning publicans and sinners, He made them see how the heavenly Father and the holy angels regarded them.

In the first two parables, those of the lost sheep and the lost coin, the Saviour Himself made the application. He said, "Likewise, I say unto you, there is joy in the presence of the angels of God over one sinner that repenteth." Man is happy when he finds some cherished possession, which was lost. So is God. Man is God's foremost creature, the object of His care and of His love. But man fell into sin, and was lost. Whenever any man, though he be the lowest of the low, is found, when he repents and returns to God, there is joy in heaven. That is the Saviour's own application of the first two parables.

In the third parable, that of the prodigal son, the Lord did not, Himself, make the application. He told the story, letting them draw their own conclusions, letting them examine their own snobbish behavior in the light of the parable. It must have been a very uncomfortable and embarrassing moment for the Pharisees.

A man had two sons. The younger, having demanded his share of the inheritance and having gone afar and spent his entire inheritance in riotous living, found himself in desperate straits. Destitute, caught in a famine, he finally was forced to accept employment as a swineherd. This, for a Jew, was contemptible beyond expression. And for payment he was permitted to eat of the food with the swine. Bitterly he thought, here am I, one of the two foremost in my father's house, where even the least of the servants enjoys good food, and I am treated as a hog. He admitted that he had deserved nothing better. He grieved not only over his own sorry plight, but over the fact that he had so grievously hurt his kind father. He repented. He returned. During the long absence the father had longed for the return of his son. And when the tramp finally came, stammering his confession, "Father, I have sinned against heaven and in thy sight, and am no more worthy to be called thy son," the father, whose heart was almost bursting with joy, hardly let him finish the sentence. He ordered a great feast to be made, and gave his son a new garment, and put a ring on his finger.

And then came an ugly incident. There stood the older brother, his face distorted with envy, complaining vehemently, because the father had made no such feast in his honor, though he had remained at home and had served his father. With abounding joy all around, there he stood muttering because the father had received back his younger son joyfully and was eating with him.

When the Saviour finished the story, He did not point an accusing finger at the Pharisees. There was no need of that. They had to apply the parable to themselves. With faces flushed with shame, they knew who was enacting the contemptible part of the elder brother. They, themselves, had just murmured because the Saviour had received publicans and sinners, prodigals who were returning to their Father's home.

The Saviour once said, "Beware of the leaven of the Pharisees, which is hypocrisy." We sing, "Jesus sinners doth receive." Nevertheless, we frequently dangerously approach the attitude of the Pharisees. We consider some people beneath us, and unworthy of our sympathy and care. We avoid them. A friendly look or word from us might change the course of their lives. May the Holy Spirit at such times remind us of this parable. Let us learn from Jesus not to let our eyes be blinded by clothes, manners, bodily cleanness, or habitation, but to see the soul for which Jesus suffered and died.

As we are by nature, we are alike in the sight of God. Dressed in royal robes or in rags—to God this means no more than it means to us when we see children playing soldier with paper hats and wooden swords. God sees the heart, and by nature all men's hearts are alike, sinful and impure. If we are different, it is only because Christ, by grace, without any merit on our part, made us different, by working faith in us, and by imputing His righteousness to us. It is His desire to do as much for all men. May we then never join in the carping and criticism of the Pharisees, but let us join in the rejoicing of the angels. May God give us grace to be of help to our Saviour in His effort to bring men to salvation. *Amen.*

# 26

## Only Hypocrites Claim
## to Live According to the Sermon
## on the Mount

### (Sixth Sunday After Trinity)
### Matthew 5:20

*For I say unto you, That except your righteousness shall
exceed the righteousness of the scribes and Pharisees, ye shall
in no case enter into the kingdom of heaven.*

It is in keeping with his character that a cloddish boor,
standing before a masterpiece in an art gallery, loudly
expresses his evaluation of it. He does so to the utter disgust
of the student of art.

In the realm of sermons, the masterpiece of all masterpieces
is our Saviour's Sermon on the Mount. No masterpiece in any
field has drawn more stupid appraisals. And they were voiced
by the learned and unlearned, by high and low, by clergy and
laity. It was the sermon which, more than any other, stirred
up the people. At its conclusion we read, "And it came to
pass, when Jesus had ended these sayings, the people were
astonished at his doctrine: for he taught them as one having
authority, and not as the scribes."

It is significant that the postscript does not read, "And the people believed on him." It was not that kind of sermon. A prerequisite of faith is the utter annihilation of every element of pride and self-righteousness. These must be so crushed by the condemnatory law of God that the haughty Pharisee, like Saul of Tarsus, will fall to the ground, and cry out, "Lord, what wilt thou have me do?" And he who has judged and condemned others, like the jailor at Philippi, will fall on his knees and stammer, "Sirs, what must I do to be saved?"

There never came a more crushing denunciation of man's sinfulness than in the Sermon on the Mount. It came as a bombshell, exploding the sham and hypocrisy of the men who posed as saints, the scribes and Pharisees. Men speak of the beauty of the Sermon on the Mount. It is beautiful, but its beauty is like that of a terrifying thunderstorm, like that of the lowering cloud of the tornado. Its purpose is to paralyze the sinner with fear, and to bring him to the brink of despair.

Daily we see people put on an air of saintliness as they boastfully tell all and sundry who will listen that they live according to the Sermon on the Mount. They are like the cloddish boor in the art gallery. They know neither what is in the Sermon of the Mount nor what is in their own hearts.

The Saviour's sermon was aimed precisely against the foolish thinking of such people. When He finished, the people said that "he taught them as one having authority, and not as the scribes." With the scribes and Pharisees everything was external. "You must not eat this or that; you must wash yourself, and your pots, and pans, and table, when you come home from the market; you must not enter the house of a gentile; you must walk no farther than a prescribed distance on the Sabbath; you must pray at certain hours, preferably in some public place; you must not actually kill someone; you must not actually steal." There were so many don'ts that no memory could contain all. They taught, "Thou shalt not kill." Our Lord branded them as murderers because they had hearts filled with hate. They taught, "Thou shalt not steal"; He burned on them the mark of the thief because their hearts were filled with envy and with a greed which moved them to devour widows' houses. With sledge-hammer blows He drove home the truth that fulfillment of the law does not consist of outward conformity to its letter, but of inward forbearance, meekness, honesty, and love.

The clan of the Pharisees is still with us. "I pattern my life after the Sermon on the Mount." When the boaster, who says that, is cornered, he will always expose his ignorance of the Sermon on the Mount and prove that he is merely living according to arbitrary standards, which he has set up for himself.

Certainly, the sincere Christian strives to conform to the Sermon on the Mount. He realizes, however, how far short he comes of what he wants to be, and of what God wants him to be. The more he reads and ponders it the more he feels his sinfulness and the need of God's forgiveness.

If men's lives were ordered into compatibility with the Sermon on the Mount, or, rather, if they could be, we would have the cure of all human ills. Wars would cease if men would heed the word of Christ, "Blessed are the peacemakers." Spiritual ignorance would soon wane if Christians could fully measure up to their Lord's esteem of them, "Ye are the light of the world." Ugly strife would no longer blight human lives if all would observe the instruction of the Master, "Leave there thy gift before the altar, and go thy way; first be reconciled to thy brother, and then come and offer thy gift." The Pharisees taught the people to love their neighbor, and to hate their enemy, but Christ insisted, "Love your enemies." And so I say again that if men's lives were ordered into compatibility with the Sermon on the Mount, we would have the cure of all ills. But this is a Utopian dream. Goodness in the human heart is an anachronism. God does not look for it there because it is not there. God does not look for goodness in the human heart; He imputes it.

Today when you reach your homes, or during the week, read the Sermon on the Mount. Read it carefully. You will find it in the fifth, sixth, and seventh chapters of Matthew. Read it slowly and see whether you can read a single sentence without being pricked in conscience. The opening sentence reads, "Blessed are the poor in spirit," those who know how poor they are spiritually, who know that in their life there is not a single deed which they could offer to God as a perfect example of their obedience to His law. The "poor in spirit" are those who are completely convinced that "all their righteousnesses are as filthy rags." Luther said, "If our salvation depended on our praying the Lord's Prayer with perfect devotion once in our lifetime, we would be damned." Are we convinced that we are so spiritually destitute? If we were, we would not be so quick to criticize others, and we would not find it so difficult to suppress that old feeling of superiority. We cannot even go beyond the first sentence in the Sermon on the Mount without the realization that we do not measure up to its demands.

In His sermon the Saviour speaks of the fowls and of the lilies. The former neither sow nor reap — come rain, come snow, come heat, come cold — "God feedeth them"; the latter toil not and spin not — no homely house dress for them — always dressed in the height of fashion — "God clothes them" as even Solomon was never arrayed in all his glory. If, the Saviour tells us, our trust in our heavenly Father were dictated by Christian common sense, we would no more be given to anxious care than are the fowls and the lilies.

Do we worrying, fretting mortals even come near to such trust in God? Look at the income of psychiatrists — they wax rich and fat on people who fret and worry until they become sick at heart and in mind. Worry is not a disease of the ignorant and primitive only — far from it, the higher men ascend the social ladder, the more educated they are, the more they worry. It comes not from a lack of learning, but from distrust in God. Can they still speak of moulding their lives to conform to the teachings of the Sermon on the Mount?

Almost every sentence in the Saviour's sermon is an indictment against us. When we give, we are not to let the left hand know what the right hand does; when we pray, we are not to parade our sanctity publicly as the Pharisees did, or make vain repetitions as the heathen do; when we are in the company of others, we are not to practice sham and hypocrisy as the Pharisees did, who applied make-up to their faces to give themselves the appearance of self-negation and fasting. Again and again the Saviour insists on purity of heart, saying that an evil tree cannot bring forth good fruit.

And now the bombshell: There in the presence of the Lord stood the scribes and Pharisees with their halos of self-righteousness, and there stood the people who were ready to admit that their goodness did not equal that of the Pharisees. It came as a rude jolt to the Pharisees and as a shock to the people when Jesus said, "Except your righteousness exceed the righteousness of the scribes and Pharisees, ye shall in no case enter into the kingdom of heaven."

Where does that leave us? The Sermon on the Mount exposes our unrighteousness as it did that of the Pharisees. Only the densest spiritual ignoramus and the most hypocritical Pharisee can say that his life is in conformity with the Sermon on the Mount. We can only join the Psalmist in his prayer, "O Lord, enter not into judgment with thy servant, for in thy sight shall no man living be justified."

No Christian sermon can end with the sermon on the Mount, but must be followed by the comforting assurance of the Gospel. The Saviour's purpose in preaching the sermon was to make His hearers fully conscious of their spiritual poverty and helplessness, and of their need of a Saviour who could supply a righteousness acceptable to God. No sermon is complete until it points the hearers to Christ, as their one and only Saviour.

Thank God for Christian mothers who taught us to pray, "Jesus, Thy blood and righteousness my beauty are, my glorious dress. Midst flaming worlds, in these arrayed, with joy do I lift up my head." Thank God for a Church which assures us, "If any man sin, we have an advocate with the Father, Jesus Christ the Righteous, and He is the propitiation for our sins, and not for ours only, but for the sins of the whole world." He purchased and won for us a perfect righteousness by the shedding of His own blood.

The Pharisees refused to accept Him. In their self-righteousness they boasted that they were not as other men are. Our Lord agreed. He separated them from others and styled them hypocrites above all other hypocrites. In their self-righteousness they felt no need of a Saviour. When thinking of heaven and salvation, let us never speak of credit for doing this or that, or of superiority over others; let us only think and speak of that which Jesus did to save us, and then, as the redeemed and saved children of God, motivated by gratitude to Him, let us earnestly try with the help of the Holy Ghost to live as He taught us in the Sermon on the Mount. *Amen.*

# 27

## Making the Blind See and the Deaf Hear, Jesus Made Us See and Hear

### (Twelfth Sunday After Trinity)
#### Mark 7:33-34

*And he took him aside from the multitude, and put his fingers into his ears, and he spit, and touched his tongue; And looking up to heaven, he sighed, and saith unto him, Ephphatha, that is, Be opened.*

When the women, who attended the national convention of the Lutheran Women's Missionary League in New York recently, returned, they spoke enthusiastically of the new school for the deaf, which our Church established not long ago. It is situated near Oyster Bay, on Long Island. Until its purchase, it was the estate of a wealthy family. There is a costly mansion in excellent repair, and there are other houses and buildings on the eighty-three-acre estate. It has all the physical equipment needed to become one of the finest schools of its kind.

In the past there was, needless to say, no intention of converting the estate into a school for the deaf. Nevertheless, that was a possibility. The possibility existed long ago, long before the estate was created, long before Long Island was discovered. In fact, the possibility existed ever since the day when Jesus opened the ears of the deaf.

The people were "beyond measure astonished" when Jesus gave hearing to the deaf man at the Sea of Galilee. No wonder, nothing like it had ever before been seen.

The human family has had its deaf members ever since the day when sin sickened man's body. And the condition of the deaf was most miserable. I am sure that any family embracing a deaf member used certain signs to inform the unfortunate one that it was time to eat, or to sleep, or to perform certain tasks. However, they must have differed with each family. There was no sign language by means of which the deaf could converse with each other, or by which they could be taught to read, or by which they could learn of the Saviour's love.

If Christ had not come, the condition of the deaf would very likely still be most miserable, even in our day. Ancient civilizations need not apologize for their advances in literature, music, and art. On the other hand, they had few charitable institutions. The weak were put to death; the lepers were driven out of the community and left to shift for themselves; the blind and deaf had no choice but to beg. There was little Christian love, and, therefore, there was little charity. Writers, artists, philosophers, theologians could boast of remarkable achievements, but physicians were heavily outnumbered by the medicine man and the witch.

Christ did not only open the ears of the deaf and the eyes of the blind; He also opened the eyes of the community and made men realize that something could be done for the blind, and deaf, and for the poor. Our new school for the deaf on Long Island, our excellent school for the deaf in Detroit, hearing aids, workshops for the blind, braille — all these are still unknown in heathen lands today, and they would be unknown here if Christ had not come and made all this possible.

Galilee had no sign language by means of which Jesus could have spoken to the deaf men. The signs mentioned in the Gospel were simply the crude signs which the deaf devised for themselves, the signs which their intimates used to

make them understand ordinary routine in daily life. I do
not know whether it was Jesus who used these signs or the
deaf man. Our English and German Bibles, with which we
are familiar, are divided into chapters and verses. Originally
they were not written in this form; nor was the same punctua-
tion used. According to our arrangement of chapters and
verses, it was Jesus who took the man aside, and put His
fingers in his ears, and spit, and touched his tongue, and
looked up to heaven. However, there is no violation of the
original text in assuming that it was the deaf man who did
all this.

We are told that he had an impediment in his speech. The
same expression also describes one man who is dumb. And
the deaf were generally dumb because there was no method
to teach them speech. It would seem, however, that this man
was completely dumb; for in their astonishment the people
said, "He maketh the deaf to hear, and the dumb to speak."

All we know is that when Jesus returned from the regions
of Tyre and Sidon to the Sea of Galilee, "they bring unto
him one that was deaf." We are not informed who "they"
were. Probably the relatives of the man. "They beseech him to
put his hand upon him." Now, it may be that Jesus then took
the man aside from the multitude, and put His fingers in
his ears, and spit, and touched his tongue, and sighed, and
looked up to heaven, in order, as some interpreters have it,
to inform him that He would now deal with him alone, that
He knew about his deafness and dumbness, sighing to remind
him of the wretched condition of sinful man, etc. But that is
not the Jesus whom we see on the many other occasions when
He healed the sick. I cannot conceive of Him using so crude
a sign language. Why should He spit? Why should He sigh
when the man could not hear the sigh, and when He Himself
knew what He would do?

The picture changes when we see the deaf man doing
all this. When his friends brought him to Jesus, he joined
in their plea. In his desire for personal attention he pulled
Jesus away from others; he put his fingers in his ears to indicate the seat of his trouble; he spit and touched his tongue
to reveal its clumsiness; he sighed, as any stricken person

would do, and pleadingly looked up to heaven. And then Jesus said, "Ephphatha, ... Be opened." "And straightway his ears were opened, and the string of his tongue was loosed, and he spake plain."

The people, "beyond measure astonished," said, "He hath done all things well." That must always be our comment when Jesus does something. He doth all things well. Those people did not fully realize how well Jesus had done that day. The echo of that omnipotent "Ephphatha" still resounds, and, in answer, ears are still being opened.

Jesus told His disciples that they, too, could perform great miracles. This promise, like His every other promise, was fulfilled and is still being fulfilled. Think of Helen Keller. As the result of an illness she became blind, deaf, and dumb at the age of nineteen months. Who could do anything for her? There was no possibility of teaching her lip-reading, because she could not see. How could she be taught to read braille? Unable to hear, she could not be told what the raised print meant. How could she be taught to use the sign language when she could neither see the signs of others, nor be told how to make them? Despite these seemingly insurmountable difficulties the miracle was performed.

By endless patience, Helen Keller's teacher, Miss Sullivan, taught her the alphabet by tracing the characters upon the palm of her hand. Stretching patience to the utmost, she taught her to distinguish the vibrations caused by the vocal chords when a word is spoken, so that Helen Keller can touch the throats of others with her fingers and feel what people say, as you hear what they say. She entered college and graduated with high honors. She fluently speaks to others by means of the sign language and reads braille without effort.

Miss Sullivan performed a mighty miracle; but Jesus had something to do with it. He made men realize that afflicted men, women, and children need not be considered as human discards. He did not give His followers the ability to perform miracles the easy way, by a mere word of power, but He gave them the wherewithal to do so the hard way, to do the seemingly impossible, as Miss Sullivan did for Helen Keller.

On Sunday afternoons, a service for the deaf is held here

in our house of worship. If you will pause to think, you will realize that you need only visit one of the services to see a miracle performed before your very eyes. In our Lord's day there were, no doubt, many God-fearing fathers and mothers in Israel who were eager to teach their deaf children the religion of God's people and to tell them of the coming Saviour. However, they were helpless. What they desired to do, they found impossible to do. Now it is being done. Unable to hear, the deaf, nevertheless, appropriate the Word of God. They read it on the lips of the preacher; they read it in the motion of his hands and expressions of his face; they read it on the printed page; just as the blind feel it when their sensitive fingers glide over the raised characters of braille.

Through our Church, and perhaps individually, we have done great things for the kingdom of God. We could do much more if we would always have the consciousness that Christ has given us power to perform miracles.

At the beginning of today's sermon I mentioned the Lutheran Women's Missionary League. It came into being when a few Christian women prayed God for enabling power to do something helpful and constructive in the great missionary enterprise of saving souls. And out of that little acorn grew a great oak. Thousands of dollars have been raised for projects undertaken in faith. And Peter was not robbed to pay Paul. The other, former, contributions of the members were not curtailed. This was something over and above their giving of the past. It is likely that of the thousands of dollars not a cent would have been given had there not in the beginning been the faith of the few. Filthy lucre has often been transformed into sanctified currency in the service of the Lord.

Always we must be mindful of the fact that He never asks us to do anything which He has not already done for us. We were spiritually blind and deaf. We could open neither our eyes nor our ears to the grace of God. The voice of the Holy Spirit penetrated through our spiritual deafness, and the rays of His inspiration pierced the blindness of our eyes. God created us; He redeemed us through the bitter suffering and death of our Saviour; He justified us through the Sanctifier, the Holy Ghost, who created in us the faith to lay hold on the merits of Jesus Christ. We are God's. We belong to Him. He has accepted us as His servants, and has endowed us with wisdom and power to do miraculous works. In grateful and humble emulation of the example of our Redeemer, who saved us and made us children of God, let us, as He did, "go about, doing good." *Amen.*

# 28

## *All of Us Are Doctor Jekyll and Mr. Hyde*

### (Fourteenth Sunday After Trinity)
#### Galatians 5:17

*For the flesh lusteth against the Spirit, and the Spirit against the flesh: and these are contrary the one to the other: so that ye cannot do the things that ye would.*

These are striking words. With my meditations on their meaning came the thought that Robert Louis Stevenson may well have had this text in mind when he wrote his novel, *Dr. Jekyll and Mr. Hyde.* It is a story of duplicity in human life.

Someone once said, "There is much goodness in the worst of us and much badness in the best of us." Nothing could be farther from the truth. Nevertheless, unthinking people repeat these words every day because catchy phrases and words appeal to them. Thus, for instance, someone called himself an "agnostic." People liked the sound of the word. Almost daily we meet people who call themselves agnostics. If the first to call himself an "agnostic" had, instead of this Greek word, used the Latin equivalent, "ignoramus," we would still have the same ignoramuses, but they would not be advertising their ignorance so happily.

Men who will tell you that "there is much good in the worst of us and much badness in the best of us" would have us believe that we can balance our faults with our virtues, and thus stand approved before God. The enlightened Christian knows how untrue this is — knows that by nature there is no good in us at all. The law of God knows no compromise. Even in the regenerate there is no balancing of good against evil. The one or the other will always hold the upper hand. "The flesh lusteth against the Spirit, and the Spirit against the flesh: and these are contrary the one to the other." We walk in the Spirit when we are led by the Spirit. On the other hand, we walk in the flesh when we are led by the flesh and do nothing that can be called good, not even if we try. The Apostle said, "Ye cannot do the things that ye would." Stevenson in his *Doctor Jekyll and Mr. Hyde* demonstrates how in the end the one always gains the supremacy over the other.

The novelist characterizes Dr. Jekyll as a reputable physician — kind, charitable, benevolent, and cheerful. By chance he concocted and swallowed a drug which transformed him into an entirely different personality, altogether evil. Under the influence of the drug he is hideous in appearance, dwarfed, and altogether contemptible; he is a monster and a fiend. After the power of the drug is dissipated, he is again Dr. Jekyll — considerate, kind, and lovable. In the end, however, he can no longer free himself from the grip of the drug, and he dies by his own hand as the fiendish Mr. Hyde.

A far more potent drug infiltrated Adam's blood when he swallowed the poisoned fruit which Satan induced him to eat. At once a complete transformation took place, from which there was no escape. He was never again a Doctor Jekyll, but forever a Mister Hyde. Gone was the image of God in which he was created; gone was the concreated righteousness and holiness. The drug of sin left him hideous and contemptible. Now, as Isaiah said, "the whole head was sick, and the whole heart faint. From the sole of the foot even unto the head there is no soundness in it; but wounds, and bruises, and putrifying sores." Like Doctor Jekyll, he had no drug powerful enough to undo the terrible mistake he had made.

He, who had fallen a prey to Satan, could not regain his status as the child of God. For him, as for Mr. Hyde, there could only be death.

But, praise be to the Lord, when man knew no transforming drug, God did. There is one medicine, and one only, which can change a child of Satan into a child of God. "The blood of Jesus Christ, his Son, cleanseth us from all sin." Here was the one drug which could resurrect man, who was already spiritually dead — the all-atoning blood of Jesus Christ.

However, it is only when man finally reaches heaven through faith in Christ Jesus that the pernicious influence of the drug of sin is completely worn off. As long as he is on this earth, the drug of sin must be counteracted by the never-ending use of the means of grace, the Gospel and the sacraments. Through these the "Spirit lusteth against the flesh." Without this antidote man cannot live spiritually. Without it Dr. Jekyll again becomes Mr. Hyde.

As a warning God holds before our eyes the example of great men of God to demonstrate how quickly the transformation can take place. Take David, for instance, the man after God's own heart. Think of him first as Doctor Jekyll. Here is the man who wrote the marvelous twenty-third psalm, not only a revelation of his own trust in God, but the source of comfort and joy for countless thousands. Here was the loving father who cried after his traitorous and murderous son, "O, Absalom, my son, my son, would God I had died for thee!" Here was the man who could take his harp and soothe the evil spirit which possessed Saul. Here was the faithful friend whose soul was knit to that of Jonathan. Here was the courageous warrior who even as a boy defended his sheep against the bear and the lion and slew the mighty Goliath. Then came the unguarded moment when he neglected the antidote against the powerful drug of sin. Now look at him, loafing on the roof of his house, casting lusting and adulterous eyes at another man's wife. Look at him now, the wife-stealer plotting the murder of her husband, Uriah, who had been one of his faithful captains. Look at him now, the ugly and impenitent Mr. Hyde. It was only because God still sought his salvation, only because the Spirit still lusted against the flesh, that finally, a year later, he was again transformed when God, through the prophet Nathan, called him to his senses.

Thus we see Peter as a Dr. Jekyll and Mr. Hyde. He was the faithful friend, the loving disciple, the noble crusader, walking to Gethsemane with his Lord, swearing that he would rather die with the Saviour than deny Him. Here was the fearless ally who drew the sword against overwhelming odds, who dared to walk upon the water when the Lord bade him do so. Think of the faith that enabled him to say, "Lord, we have toiled all the night and taken nothing, but at thy word I will let down the net." Here was the man who gave utterance to the never-to-be-forgotten words, "Lord, to whom shall we go? Thou hast the words of eternal life"; and, on another occasion, "Thou art the Christ, the Son of the Living God." Then came the hour when "the flesh lusted against the Spirit," when the fire of coals appeared warmer than the love of Christ. Is that the same Peter, the same bold and strong man, that contemptible Mr. Hyde, who is cringing in terror before the accusing finger of a maid? Is that the man of the wonderful confession, whose lips are uttering the foul curses? Is that the same Peter, who drew the sword in defense of his Master, now swearing that he does not know Him and wants nothing to do with Him? Yes, it is the same Peter. Only the fact that even then the Saviour's love was the most powerful force on earth caused him to go forth, weeping bitterly, as he repented of his denial.

Abraham, Jonah, Solomon, Paul, and all other great believers are witnesses for the fact that the struggle between the Spirit and the flesh never ceases, so long as the child of God is on this earth. We see them rise to great heights of faith, and we see them fall to abysmal depths of unbelief and sin.

Bismarck, the great statesman, confessed that he was no exception and that the conflict between the Spirit and the flesh raged in his heart. He said, "Would God that I had no other sins than those which are known to my fellow men."

Why look to others? The proof lies within us. We are constantly disquieted and torn by the struggle in our hearts. The flesh, our sinful nature, is in constant rebellion against the Spirit. Heeding the Spirit, we appear as Doctor Jekyll, under the influence of Word and Sacrament. We kneel at the altar on the day of our confirmation and make a noble confession, even as Peter did. We work and contribute for the building of Christ's kingdom; we are kind, charitable, and sincere. And then come unguarded moments, when we neglect the means of grace, when we become veritable Mr. Hydes. All too often we have reason to say with Bismarck, "Would God I had no other sins than those which are known to my fellow men."

It follows, of course, that only the completely spiritually blind can prattle of balancing their good deeds against the evil deeds. All the virtues of the lovable Dr. Jekyll could not balance his evil deeds as Mr. Hyde, not even in the scales of man's justice; for had he been caught, he would have been hanged. In the case of David, all the beauty of his character, seen through his twenty-third psalm, was hideously distorted by his sins of adultery and murder. Of that he himself was fully aware. For an entire year he did not even dare to pray. Peter's conscience cut short any notion that his fine words could atone for his cursing and denying. Hence his emphatic statement at a later date, "For ye know that ye were not redeemed with corruptible things, as silver and gold, from your vain conversation received by tradition from your fathers; but with the precious blood of Christ, as of a lamb without blemish and without spot."

Paul says, "So that ye cannot do the things that ye would." Nightly, in our prayers, we plead God's forgiveness and promise to amend, only to admit the next evening that it was a day like every other day, a day of sin in thought, word, deed, and desire. Our flesh is never completely rid of the drug of sin. It works on and on, always seeking to revert us to our lost condition. Greatly as we may desire to do good, we daily do things that are evil.

Again, it follows that if we cannot do what we would, then we must find someone who can. And there is only One, the Spirit, who never ceases to lust against the flesh. We must daily use the antidote which the Spirit prescribes for us, the Word and the Sacrament. And, of ourselves, we have no inclination to make use of them; so even that must be instilled in us by the Spirit. Let us look away from any imaginary good in us and turn to the Spirit and to our Saviour. Let us turn to the one with the sincere prayer, "Create in me a clean heart, O God, and renew a right spirit within me"; and let us turn to the other with a humble and contrite heart, saying,

> *Nothing in my hands I bring,*
> *Simply to Thy Cross I cling.*

*Amen.*

# 29

## *Only Thinking People Are Thankful People*

### (Fourteenth Sunday After Trinity)
### Luke 17:17

*And Jesus answering said, Were there not ten cleansed? but where are the nine?*

On a day in His busy ministry the Saviour happened to come to a leper colony. Perhaps my words are not well chosen. He did not just happen to come. We might say, one day the Saviour happened to pass through Jericho. We know, however, He did not just happen to pass through. He had to attend to the Father's business in Jericho. He said to Zacchaeus, "This day I must abide in thy house." The word "must" precludes the thought that He came by mere chance. It was not a mere accidental meeting when He came to the city gate of Nain at the very moment when the people were bearing the body of the widow's son to the cemetery. When Lazarus died, Christ told His disciples that his illness and death was for the glory of God. The resurrection of Lazarus was planned and timed. And so it also was not mere chance when He came to the lepers. He came there because they were there.

It was a great day for the leper colony. Had he not come,

a slow and torturous death would have awaited them. As we picture the scene, we can hardly believe that only one of the ten returned to give thanks after they had been so miraculously healed.

The Holy Spirit did not record this miracle merely to show us that Christ could cure even lepers, but to make us realize how few people are thankful. One in ten. But for the fact that the one who returned was a Samaritan, there might not even have been one in ten. To him it was most astounding that Jesus should manifest interest in him at all. He would not have been greatly surprised if Jesus had healed the other nine and ignored him; for Jews usually did not even speak to Samaritans. That the nine Jews had tolerated the Samaritan in their midst is not too surprising; for they were all facing death, and death is the great leveler. Cultural and racial prejudices fade away in the great democracy of death.

One in ten — not a very cheerful observation. On Thanksgiving Day we sing, "Come, ye thankful people, come." If only the truly thankful came, there would be no large attendance.

It costs so little effort to give thanks. We sometimes use the expression, "I am indebted to you." When someone is kind to us, a debt is imposed upon us. We owe it to our benefactor to thank him. If nothing else, our own experience should make us aware of our duty to give thanks. It grieves us when others are ungrateful to us. It happened again and again that people whom I instructed and confirmed, for whom I found employment, at whose beck and call I visited them in sickness and trouble, asked for a dismissal to another congregation. And then they left without even saying good-by, much less uttering a word of thanks. It hurt until I told myself, it serves you right, for often you failed to give thanks to God for much greater favors.

One in ten. Can it be possible that for ten favors received from God we give thanks for only one? Yes, it is possible; it is possible; it is even likely. And perhaps our record is even worse.

Jesus did not come to the lepers by mere chance, nor did He come to our assistance by chance. We were in a worse dilemma than the lepers. We were stricken with the leprosy of sin. And we could do no more to help ourselves than they could. We could not cure ourselves of sin. That meant not only temporal death, it meant eternal death. It meant damnation, and an eternity of suffering. Then came Jesus. Not by mere chance. Oh, no, He and the Father had counseled together far back in eternity and had planned our salvation. He had compassion on us. When there was only one way,.the way of the agonizing cross, He did not hesitate to give His very life as our ransom.

It is true, not a Sunday passes by but what we render thanks in prayer and hymns. However, voicing thanks and feeling thankful are two different things. Naturally, we cannot look into the hearts of others and see who is thankful and who is not. But we can weigh the outward evidence. We can see the church attendance, and observe the communion record, and count the contributions. We may not know whether a person is feverish merely by his looks, but the thermometer will tell the story. And these outward evidences also tell a story.

Nor do we owe thanks to God only for our salvation. Every sentence in our Christian Creed mentions an item for which we owe thanks to God. Jesus is our Helper not only in spiritual need, but in bodily need as well. He has said, "Call upon me in the day of trouble, and I will deliver thee." We do that. We call upon Him when we are in trouble, when we are sick, when we are unemployed, when we are in need. But He did not merely say, "I will deliver thee." He also said, "And thou shalt glorify me." He expects that from us. There are many other words of Holy Writ which make it our duty to give thanks. Too often we fail.

Why are we not as grateful to God as we should be? Look into your own heart. Only you and God know what the thoughts of your heart are. You know yourself better than anyone else can know you. If you examine yourself closely you will, no doubt, find the reasons for your ungratefulness. On the other hand, we all are so much alike that what is true of the one is generally true of the other also. What rendered the nine lepers ungrateful renders us ungrateful also.

The Gospel does not tell us why they did not return to Jesus. It only tells us that they did not, and that Jesus was disappointed and grieved. With profound sadness He asked, "Were there not ten cleansed, but where are the nine?"

Their failure to return was due to motives which under other circumstances would not have been open to criticism. No doubt, they were eager to hasten to their homes to embrace their loved ones. Who could blame them for that? I am sure they longed to sit at the family table and to eat a home-cooked meal. Who could find fault with them for that? They were unquestionably anxious to return to their occupation and business, so long neglected. Why not? Nevertheless, there was one obligation which should have come first. They should have returned to pour out their thanks to Jesus. They should have remembered that all their desires which were now about to be gratified would have remained unanswered, had Jesus not cured them. In their elation over the outlook of better days ahead, they did not think how disappointed their Healer would be. Did Jesus condone their ingratitude? He did not. He voiced His disapproval when He said, "Were there not ten cleansed, but where are the nine?"

For my own satisfaction I consulted my concordance to see how often the Bible speaks of thinking and of meditating. Jesus asked, "How think ye?" "What think ye?" "What think ye of Christ?" The Psalmist says, "I will meditate also of all thy work."

God thinks of us. The Psalmist says, "How wonderful are thy thoughts to me, O God." God Himself says, "I know the thoughts that I think towards you, thoughts of peace, and not of evil." We are always in the thoughts of God. He thinks of what He can give us, and of what He can do for us and for our salvation. Should we not think of Him, and of what we owe Him?

In this respect there is a difference between oriental people and occidental people. In the orient it is a common thing to see people sit down to think and to meditate. It is easy, for instance, to engage an Arab in conversation if you will talk to him of his soul and of peace with God. They lag behind us in their thinking along material lines — in medical research, in chemical research, etc. But are these more important than matters that pertain to the soul? Are they as important as our relationship to God?

In a way, a moron is, in a sense, happy because there is so little to disturb him on the very narrow plane of his existence. But truly happy people are people who are happy in God, people who know what God has done for them, and still does for them daily, people who have meditated on the works of God, and who are truly thankful to God for planning their temporal life and their eternal life.

This morning we have been thinking collectively. If there is anyone here who, after these moments, thinks he is as thankful toward God as he should be, I want to apologize to him for having wasted his time. But we, who must shamefully admit that we are too much like the "nine" who failed to return to give thanks, let us not cease to think about this. Let us ask the Holy Spirit to sanctify our thoughts so that we may think clearly, and become ever more thankful to Him who "forgiveth all our iniquities, and healeth all our diseases." Amen.

# 30

## Every Man's Question: Shall It Be God or Mammon?

(Fifteenth Sunday After Trinity)
Matthew 6:24

*No man can serve two masters: for either he will hate the one, and love the other; or else he will hold to the one, and despise the other. Ye cannot serve God and mammon.*

Ye cannot serve God and mammon." Noteworthy commentators have surmised that people in our Lord's day knew a heathen idol by the name of Mammon, and that he was the god of riches. Milton, in "Paradise Lost," thus names one of the angels who was expelled from heaven in the company of Satan. We have neither the corroboration of history for the existence of an idol called Mammon, nor that of the Bible for a fallen angel named Mammon.

Nevertheless, mammon is the idol of many nations — worshipped by Americans, Englishmen, Russians, Japanese, Hottentots, and Australian Bushmen. Nor was it far-fetched when Milton gave the name to a fallen angel. Mammon is a fallen angel. Riches — gold, silver, precious stones, real estate — were all part of God's wonderful creation, designed for the enjoyment of man and for his use in the adoration and worship of his Creator. But man subverted the gifts of God and dissipated them as he aspired to the throne of God. Riches became both a god and a fallen angel; and men became idolators.

In our catechism we speak of two forms of idolatry — gross idolatry and fine idolatry. It is gross idolatry when men actually worship and adore a creature as god, when heathen people bow before idols of wood and stone, when they pay divine homage to the sun, or moon, or sacred bulls, or saints. God has said, "I am the Lord, that is my name, and my glory will I not give to another."

On the other hand, it is fine idolatry when men fear, love, or trust a creature as they should fear, love, and trust only the Lord. Of the two, the second is the worst because it is more insidious, more refined, and at the same time more capable of foul and fiendish deeds. Men are not at their worst when they put on a mask to rob a bank. When they perform their dirtiest deals, they put on "white tie and tails," or a uniform, or even a red hat.

The gross idolator is readily distinguished from the Christian by his outward actions when he kneels before a graven image or statue. The fine idolator, on the other hand, is often disguised as a philanthropist, as a paragon of virtue, as a priest bearing a crucifix.

"No man can serve two masters." The Saviour says, "he will hate the one and love the other." The word '"hate" here means to love less. In this sense it is often used in Scripture. "Jacob loved Rachel, but hated Leah." He loved Leah less than Rachel. God Himself said, "Jacob have I loved, but Esau have I hated." The context reveals the meaning. God gave the posterity of Jacob, the Jews, far more privileges and opportunities than He gave the posterity of Esau, the Edomites. He loved the Israelites more than the Edomites. Thus men love riches more than God. Men cannot have the same affection for two objects which are incompatible. What he loves the most is his god.

Hundreds and hundreds of proverbs have been coined concerning riches. A proverb is a striking or witty saying, spoken in praise, or pity, or contempt, and so often repeated that it becomes a proverb. A proverb speaks of something firmly believed, or greatly admired, or utterly despised. Many proverbs deal with riches. "A ready penny is as good a friend as any." This proverb bespeaks the opinion of many that money is worthy of their trust. "Add pence to pence, for wealth comes hence." This one makes wealth the object of man's striving. "A fool and his money are soon parted." So, a wealthy man must be a wise man. As has been said, hundreds of such sayings give voice to the innermost convictions of the mammon servants. There are just as many which express the opposite persuasion. "Rather be rich in good than to be rich in goods." Worldly people envy the rich who possess much goods while we far more admire those who do much good. Another proverb reads, "Riches have made more men covetous than covetousness has made men rich." Men covet riches and as they grow rich, they grow more covetous. "Riches make to themselves wings, and fly away." And to this Spurgeon adds, "Do not let yours fly away, but clip their wings, and send the feathers to an orphanage, or other charity."

Such proverbs show how many people — enlightened or barbarian — in any nation worship mammon, and they show how many realize what a deceitful and false god mammon is.

Mammon is a god who can adjust himself to changing conditions as well as to the thinking of people. As a rule, when the weakness and the unreality of an idol are exposed, the idol topples from his throne. For centuries the Japanese people worshiped their emperor as a god. However, when the nation was defeated in war and the emperor barely escaped trial as a war criminal, his subjects no longer deified him. When Christianity conquered, Baal, Jupiter, and a host of gods were exiled to the realm of the myth. But mammon is a god who rebounds from any setback. Think how he adjusted himself to the change in our national thinking. From the birth of our nation to recent times a savings account was stressed. Everybody was urged to save for a rainy day and for old age. Conformity to this thought made misers of many. They hoarded their gains, and their hearts delighted in the growth of their bank account. With the emergence of the new conception that the government owes the citizens a living and that the government must provide for the old age of its subjects, came Social Security and Old Age Pension. And with these came the era of spending. Why save for old age? The government will provide. But, did people stop the worship of mammon? No, he is more firmly enthroned now than before. We have had more strikes; we have had a steady increase in crime. Recently a gangster boasted of his wealth — so great, he said, that he could buy the entire Justice Department. No, mammon is one god who will not abdicate his throne to the end of time.

In the days of Elijah many people rendered lip service to the true God, while they joined in the worship of Baal. They were challenged by Elijah with his taunting question, "How long halt ye between two opinions?" "Ye walk like people who are lame in both legs. First ye tilt to one side and then to the other. Walk straight! Come out in the open! Either acknowledge that ye are servants of Baal, and renounce the true God; or serve God, and renounce Baal."

This challenge of Elijah is repeated by Christ, saying, "Ye cannot serve God and mammon." He, too, is asking, "Why halt ye between two opinions. Make up your minds. Which shall it be, God or mammon?"

For our warning and for our example the Bible introduces us to men who were rich in goods only, and also to men who were rich in good. I do not, by any means, intend to imply that the servants of mammon are found only among the rich. Some of the worst are among the poor. Judas was one of these. He was a penny-snatcher who snitched pennies from the little household money of the disciples, which was entrusted to him. In the end he betrayed his Lord for the paltry sum of thirty pieces of silver. Among the most contemptible of the mammon servants mentioned in the Bible was the miser, whose crop exceeded the capacity of his barns. Conversing with himself, he said, "This will I do: I will pull down my barns, and build greater; . . . and I will say to my soul, Soul, thou hast much goods laid up for many years; take thine ease, eat, drink, and be merry." A more honorable mammon servant was the rich young ruler, who asked the Lord to accept Him as as disciple. But, whether they are pikers, like Judas; or plutocrats, like the rich miser; or socially elite, like the young ruler; the end is the same — Judas hanged himself, the miser had a stroke, and the younger ruler was discredited. Of such the Bible says, "It is easier for a camel to pass through the eye of a needle than for a rich man to enter heaven."

On the other hand, for our example, the Bible introduces us to men and women who were rich in good. Numbered among these are some whose benevolent activity was restricted to their own community; some who reached out much farther; and a few who embraced all parts of the world. Mary anointed the Saviour with the costly spikenard; Dorcas sewed for the poor in Joppa; the good Samaritan dispensed his oil and wine; Paul traveled hither and yon, bringing the saving Gospel to men. But whether their work was of a local or of a global nature, in the end there was the benediction, "Blessed are the dead which die in the Lord from henceforth: Yea, saith the Spirit, that they may rest from their labors; and their works do follow them."

The highest and noblest example of being rich in good was set for us by our Saviour. For our sakes He became the poorest of the poor; but in this respect He was the richest of the rich. "He went about doing good"—that sums up His life. In earthly goods He possessed only His garments and His sandals; and in the end even these were taken from Him when the soldiers made them the stake of their gambling under the cross. But there on the cross, when He died in utter poverty and naked-ness He became rich, far beyond all human calculation. Now came the reward of which Isaiah spoke in the thrilling words, "He shall see of the travail of his soul, and shall be satisfied; by his knowledge shall my righteous servant justify many; for he shall bear their iniquities. Therefore will I divine him a portion with the great, and he shall divide the spoil with the strong; because he hath poured out his soul unto death." The endless number of those who are dressed in white robes, who have come out of great tribulation to sing His praises before His throne, because He enabled them to wash their garments white in His blood — these are His reward for a life spent in doing good; above all, for sacrificing Himself as an offering for the sin of the world.

For you there can now be no neutrality. It must be the one

or the other; it must be Christ or mammon. Will you stand with Judas, with the miser, with the young ruler, or will you stand with Mary, with Dorcas, and with Paul? There is no middle ground. "Ye cannot serve God and mammon." Whom will you serve? May the Holy Spirit help you to give the right answer. *Amen.*

# 31

## Miracles Without Number

### (Nineteenth Sunday After Trinity)
#### Matthew 9:2

*And, behold, they brought to him a man sick of the palsy, lying on a bed: and Jesus seeing their faith said unto the sick of the palsy; Son, be of good cheer; thy sins be forgiven thee.*

According to John, Jesus performed so many miracles that the books of the world cannot contain them. Had he not written this by divine inspiration, we might think this an overstatement. This means, of course, that the great majority of our Lord's miracles are not recorded in Holy Writ. Only miracles which substantiated a particular Christian doctrine, or threw light on Christian practice, are preserved for our learning.

In our Christian Creed we confess, "I believe in the resurrection of the dead." For the strengthening of our faith in this doctrine the Bible recorded the resurrection of the young man at Nain, of the daughter of Jairus, of Lazarus, and of Christ Himself. We confess, "I believe in the forgiveness of sin." To corroborate this teaching our text brings this miracle and several others in which Jesus healed not only physical illness but spiritual illness as well. We believe that God is not only the almighty Maker, but also the absolute Ruler of all nature, and the Preserver of mankind. In proof the Bible tells us of the Saviour's power to still the tempest, to feed multitudes with a few loaves and fishes, and it tells us how He cursed the fig tree, which immediately withered and died.

However, the miracles which are recorded in the Bible to vindicate the Saviour's claim to divinity, to substantiate doctrines, and to teach us our proper relationship to God and our fellow men are only a very small, though carefully selected, handful of the many, many miracles our Lord performed. You have, no doubt, seen some buyer of cotton, tobacco, or grain judge the whole by a handful. The buyer of wool, for instance, will reach deep into a sack and extract a handful, which he tests and whereby he judges the entire sack. And so the Bible selects, as it were, a handful of our Saviour's miracles, whereby we are to judge His grace, love, and power, as well as His attitude toward poor sinners, including ourselves.

No one will ever know how many miracles our Lord performed. Reaching Capernaum one evening, He found Peter's mother-in-law laid low with a fever. No sooner had He healed her when she arose and waited on Him and His disciples at table. The news spread like wildfire. The meal had hardly been concluded before many of the sick in Capernaum had been carried as near to Peter's house as the throng permitted. "And he healed them all." Capernaum was the largest of the cities bordering on the Sea of Galilee. Picture to yourself how many deaf, blind, sick, and crippled people are found in any good-sized town of America today, despite all the forward strides taken by medicine. "And he healed them all."

Matthew writes that "great multitudes followed him, and he healed all their sick." When news spread that Jesus was approaching by a certain road, multitudes converged on that road, bringing their sick, maimed, and afflicted, setting them down by the roadside, waiting for Jesus to come and heal them.

It was not until 1889 that the first appendectomy was performed. In my boyhood days even we children were familiar with the term "inflammation of the bowels," because that was so frequently given as the cause of death." Now we know, many died of appendicitis. Then came the first operation. For the next several years the newspapers still made much of a successful appendectomy. Many still died. I have seen scars as mementos of those early operations. They spoke of the clumsiness of surgeons. Today it is only a question of reaching a hospital on time. Before the week is over, the patient is back home.

In our Saviour's day it was only a question of getting to Him. Appendicitis, cancer, gall stones, polio, leukemia, deafness, blindness — "He healed them all." We read, "Jesus went through all Galilee,... healing the sick,... and his fame went throughout all Syria; and they brought ... their sick,... and he healed them." Syria comprised not only all of Palestine, but surrounding territories as well. Without trains, automobiles, buses, etc., it must have been a considerable hardship to bring the sick so great a distance. But many thousands did, "and he healed them." No wonder John tells us the world did not have sufficient books to contain all His miracles.

In the Gospel for today we read to what end people went to bring their sick to Jesus. "They brought to him a man sick of the palsy, lying on a bed." Mark tells us Jesus was in a house so filled with people that the friends of the palsied man could not get near the door. Undaunted, they carried him to the roof of the house and lowered him to the feet of Jesus, as we lower a man to his grace. All hindrances were overcome by people who were determined to bring their sick to Jesus.

Picture your Saviour in those days, as He walked over the highways of Palestine, lined with the sick and afflicted. He stretched forth His hand, now to the right, now to the left, "and he healed them all."

But while Jesus healed the sick and raised the dead, He did not do away with sickness and death; for these came into the world with sin and will remain to the end of time because sin will remain to the end of time. All the sick whom Jesus healed died later, because that is the fate of all mankind. Jesus healed the sick to prove Himself the Messiah, and because He had compassion on men.

And still He heals the sick in answer to prayer. As we do not know how many people Jesus healed when He was on earth, so we do not know how many He has healed since then in answer to prayer, nor do we know how many He is healing in our day in answer to prayer.

We are living in an era of medical research. Scientists are searching for remedies for cancer, tuberculosis, arthritis, and other killers. How often have you prayed that God may lead them to the cure? Have you prayed at all for their success? The Saviour's miracles came in response to prayer of some kind. Sometimes there were loud voices. The lepers cried, "Jesus, Master, have mercy on us." The more people tried to silence him, the louder blind Bartimaeus shouted, "Jesus, thou son of David, have mercy on me." Sometimes it was prayer in the form of deep desire, as when the woman said to herself, "If I can touch the hem of his garment, I shall be healed." Sometimes there was only a beseeching look, as when the paralyzed man looked up to Jesus from his bed. Always His ear was sensitive to prayer. And He still hears the prayer of the sick.

In one respect especially has our Saviour not changed. He is still the same Jesus who once said, "Son, be of good cheer, thy sins be forgiven thee."

When countless thousands brought their sick to Jesus, and He healed them all, the priests, scribes, and Pharisees turned green with envy. Hitherto the people had looked to them. In case of illness they brought a sacrifice — a dove, a lamb, and sometimes money. There was a handsome profit in first selling a sacrificial animal to the worshipper and then claiming a part of it as a priest's emolument. There was also a considerable profit in the exchange rate; for worshippers had to convert their currency into temple money. Now business was bad and profits were shrinking. Hitherto people had appealed to the priests to settle religious disputes; now they were ignored — everybody was going to Jesus. Worse still, they had to keep silent. It was the time of our Lord's greatest popularity, and the people were not in a mood to tolerate any bickering on the part of Jesus' enemies.

However, even silence could not save the priests and Pharisees from exposure. The Saviour read their hearts like an open book. When, on this occasion, the Saviour said to the paralyzed man, "Son, be of good cheer, thy sins be forgiven thee," they said in their hearts, "This man blasphemeth." In the presence of the people they did not dare to say it aloud. How embarrased they were when Jesus looked at them and said, "Wherefore think ye evil in your hearts? For whether is easier to say, Thy sins be forgiven thee; or to say, Arise and walk?" They did not dare to answer. They knew what was coming. They knew that only God had the right to say, "Thy sins be forgiven thee; and they knew that only God could substantiate His right to say it by the power to say, "Arise and walk." And then Jesus did say, "Arise, take up thy bed, and go unto thine house."

In the Saviour's day there were those who brought the sick to Jesus; there were the priests and Pharisees, who sought to prevent them; and I am sure there was a third class; namely, the indifferent and selfish people, who did not lend a helping hand to bring people to Jesus.

We have the same three classes. As then, so today, there are those who seek to prevent people from coming to the Saviour. And I am not now thinking of communistic Russians and Red Chinese, but of Americans who are the foes of Christ. There are today millions of selfish and indifferent people, who never think of the spiritual woes of others. But, thank God, there are also those who will go to any end to bring men to Jesus, even as the men in today's Gospel brought the paralyzed man.

To which group do you belong? You do belong to one of the three. We bring men to Jesus by personal evangelism — by inviting someone to attend the church serivce, by bringing a child to Sunday School, by leading a Christian life. And we bring men to Jesus by contributing to the missionary work of the church. Thus you give poor sinners the opportunity to hear the most wonderful words that can be spoken, "Son, be of good cheer; thy sins be forgiven thee."

What you do to bring men to Christ will always depend on how much you appreciate what Christ has done for you. If you want to be saved merely because you do not want to be damned, then you are like a man who wants to marry a woman, any woman, because he does not wish to be alone.

Such a man will bestow little love on his wife. But if your heart is filled with gratitude and love because Jesus has saved you, there will be no coldness and indifference toward others. And Jesus did save you. To that end He came into the world; to that end He labored until He could finally say, "It is finished." All that remains is for us to accept what He so freely offers. But then there will also be a willingness to share with others. As He once was the only one who could do what He did, so He is still the only one in whom men can find salvation. Bring them to Jesus. Let nothing stop you. *Amen.*

# 32

## *Your Life — Not What Belongs to You, But Whom You Belong To*

### (Reformation)
### Luke 12:15

*And he said unto them, Take heed ... for a man's life consisteth not in the abundance of the things which he possesseth.*

(This sermon was preached at Concordia College, Fort Wayne, Ind., in a Reformation service, held jointly by the congregations of the Lutheran Church, Missouri Synod, in October, 1948.)

A few weeks ago I attended a meeting in Pittsburgh, in which one of the speakers related that he was present at the opening ceremonies of the Olympic games in England this past summer. "Eighty-three thousand people," he said, "had filled the huge stadium to its capacity. The king had entered the royal box on the opposite side of the field; and then the procession of the athletes of the participating nations began, according to their alphabetical order, beginning with Argentina. As each contingent entered there was applause, especially when Australia, Canada, and New Zealand made their appearance. Finally, way at the last, came the contestants from our own country. At the first glimpse of "Old Glory" coming through the gates of the stadium the entire assembly arose as one man. Louder and louder grew the cheering as the several hundred young American men and women dressed in their spotless uniforms of blue and white marched behind our flag in perfect precision." The speaker said that he was unashamed of the tears that trickled over his face. "Never before," said he, "did I feel so deeply that the most important thing in life is not what belongs to you, but what you belong to."

Nineteen hundred years ago, our Lord and Saviour stood upon the earth and said, "A man's life consisteth not in the abundance of the things which he possesseth." He, too, was saying, "The most important thing in life is not what belongs to you, but what you belong to." Reformation Day is a proper time to let this truth sink deeply into our minds and hearts.

It would, of course, be utter folly to say that our material possessions are not important to us. They are. Your home, your business, your farm, your money, your car, your radio, your jewels, your clothes — all these things are important to you and are a part of your life. But they are not your life. If there were nothing else, your life would be lonely and empty indeed. Your real life consists not of what belongs to you, but of what you belong to.

You belong to your family, to which you are bound by ties of love so strong that even death cannot completely sever them. You belong to societies and organizations through which the noblest thoughts of your soul find their expression. You belong to the United States of America, and what a privilege it is that you can breathe its air of freedom! You belong to the Lutheran Church, and in that membership lies the secret of your spiritual liberty. These are the things, the things to which you belong, which are your very life.

We Lutherans of America have a twofold creed: We proudly stand before the world, together with all patriotic Americans, and say, "I believe in the flag of the United States, and in the republic for which it stands." And we unite with all true Lutherans in the confession, "I believe in the Lutheran Church, and in her platform, and Augsburg Confession." The fourth of July and the thirty-first of October are both our Independence Days.

I am an American. I am a citizen of the greatest and most wonderful country in the world. Do not think that I am making some kind of Fourth of July speech. When you say, "I am an American," you should say it with reverence, with awe, and with a deep sense of gratitude to God. Think of its size! I have driven my car through every state of the United States, and in those vast open spaces of our West the thought came again and again, "We could invite all the dispossessed people of Europe and never know that they are here." Think of the wealth of our country! We squandered and wasted unbelievable sums of money in our conduct of the war, and yet so limitless are our wealth and natural resources that we simply overwhelmed our enemies, despite the fact that they used far greater discretion and prudence in their household. Think of the freedom in our country! We are the envy of the world. Those millions of Russian peasants who had their homesteads confiscated and who were incorporated in the collective farm system, no doubt cried out in the anguish of their hearts, "God forbid that I should give thee the inheritance of my fathers." But, like Naboth, they were silenced by ruthless and brutal dictatorship. The thousands of Russians in forced labor camps; the thousands who were herded into Siberia without a hearing; and the thousands of women and children who did not dare to protest when their dear ones were shot down without a trial — how they long for the freedom which we Americans take for granted. Perhaps, if we were deprived of our liberty for a while, away from the freedom we have we too, would cry out as did the returning soldier who, when coming in from the sea, saw the Statue of Liberty and said, "Old girl, if you ever want to see me again, you will have to turn around."

Do you know why you enjoy the freedom which makes us the envy of the world? Because Christ once stood upon the earth and taught men the dignity of the individual as a child of God, created in His image, and because there was once a Martin Luther whose titanic assertion that all men should be free to worship God according to the dictates of their own consciences gave back to the world the conception of the dignity of the individual, which Christ proclaimed. As an American citizen you are not a mere cog in a political machine, built and run by a political overlord to whom you mean no more than a nut or a bolt; but you are an individual, free, and as untrammelled as the President of the United States himself. You have a voice in government, and you can demand the protection of your government, not only within the bounds of our own country, but on foreign soil as well. Your government will hold anyone to strict accountability for any harm that is done to you while abroad. Even if you do that which is wrong, your country will insist that you be given a fair trial and that your rights be protected. For you are an American, with whose freedom no one dare triffle.

Under God you owe that to Martin Luther who gave back to the world this conception of the dignity of the individual. Martin Luther and the heroic figures who stood on the burning pyres of Europe, they must ever in our eyes stand at the side of Thomas Jefferson and George Washington and the other patriots to whom we owe our freedom.

When Luther, as a nine-year-old boy, heard that Columbus had sailed away on the boundless sea, he could not have dreamed that God was leading Columbus to the discovery of the land where the freedom should find fertile soil—soil which began to germinate sixteen years later when Luther nailed his ninety-five theses to the door of the castle church in Wittenberg.

Recently, *Life* concluded its article, "The Protestant Revolution," with the words, "Nor did the energy of the new Spirit stop with the sixteenth century or the continent of Europe. It leaped the Atlantic Ocean and prepared to clear a continental forest and made appropriate space where the dignity of the individual, safeguarded by his new freedom of faith could, under God, build a citadel, an arsenal, and an altar."

You belong to America. Thank God for that; and do not forget that the freedom which makes life worth-while, and which allows you to pursue your happiness without the crushing impact of dictatorship (which would order your private life, your thinking, your planning, and your endeavor) is something which, under God, you owe to Martin Luther. You can voice your own opinion; you can send your child to the school of your own choice; you can buy a house or sell it; you can work where you please and do business with whom you please; you can travel without restriction and go where you please; all this because you belong to America. Where dictatorship rules, man is considered worth no more than the ox or the ass. Where freedom rules, the dignity of the individual is preserved. And on this earth freedom reigns today only where the light of the Reformation is allowed to shine.

You belong to the Lutheran Church. This does not merely mean that you hold membership in the Lutheran Church. It means far more than that. It means that you can enjoy to the fullest the spiritual freedom which Christ won for us and of which He said, "If the Son therefore shall make you free, ye shall be free indeed." And this spiritual freedom God also restored to us through Martin Luther. Christ brought freedom not only from the bondage of the ceremonial law under which the people of the old covenant had groaned, but He brought freedom from the slavery of sin and of Satan.

When man came forth from the hand of his Creator, he was a free man, indeed. He was clothed with royal dignity. God set him to have dominion over all the earth and to subdue it. In the order of creation, God had made him only a little lower than the angel. His was not only the good will of God but the love of God. He had free access to God. His was the happy relationship of a royal prince to his father, the King. Why should we be surprised today that there are dupes in our country, misguided souls, with warped minds, who are ready to surrender the freedom of America to crawl under the vile and wicked rule of communism? Man, in the freedom of paradise, did far worse than that. He departed from God, abased himself, and subjected himself to the slavery of sin and Satan. Too late he realized his folly. Degraded by sin, a slave to Satan, he could not regain his liberty. But in his boundless mercy God sent His Son to fight the war for spiritual independence against Satan. It was a terrific battle. It brought the Christ of Heaven down to the dust of Gethsemane, where under the accusation of His conscience He was shaken and pounded until in His agony He cried, "O God, can't you let up, is there not some other way?" It brought Him to the cross, where the hideousness and nakedness of sin was exposed as never before, until in that foul-smelling sulphur of a burning hell He cried, "My God, my God, why hast thou forsaken me?" But He won the battle. And glorious was the light of freedom that shone forth with the rising of the Easter Sun.

And again man almost completely surrendered that hard-won freedom during the dark ages when a corrupt church substituted a corrupt religion for the beautiful religion of Christ, and again, slavery for freedom. The religion of Luther's youth was slavery, a religion of fear and superstition, so comfortless, so devoid of assurance and certainty that it brought Luther to the very brink of despair. The hierarchy of that day taught Christianity as a system of moral laws, of commandments, of compulsion, and of prohibitions, a religion as unlike that which Christ taught as night is different than day.

That was the religion of Luther's youth. No wonder! He never saw the Bible until he was twenty years old. Time does not permit me to describe in detail how Luther, whom God had chosen as the leader of the coming revolution, battled his way through the pestilential bog of false doctrines and superstition to the light of the truth. Suffice it to say that for him life began with an understanding of the doctrine of justification by grace, through faith; without the deeds of the law. It was through the Bible that God led him to spiritual freedom, and it was through the Bible that Luther led the church out of the Babylonian captivity, back to the promised land of liberty.

And now you belong to the Lutheran Church. And what this means was beautifully expressed by the Apostle Paul, when he said, "You are Christ's and Christ is God's." As Christ is one with Father, so you are one with Christ. "I am the vine, ye are the branches." As the Father revealed Himself through Christ, so Christ reveals Himself to the world through you. Through you He does His work here on earth. You are bound to Him by the same intimacy by which He is bound to the Father. You are a child of God, an heir of eternal life. You are made sure of your inheritance in heaven.

It may help you to appreciate what membership in the Lutheran Church means to you if you picture to yourself two men on their death beds. To the one comes a priest whose teaching of the beautiful Gospel of Christ is obscured, dimmed, and besmirched by the teaching of a miserable self-righteousness. He brings with him the paraphernalia for a final unction. He speaks and says, "I must tell you that you are, as soon as you close your eyes, about to enter upon a time of terrible suffering. You are going to purgatory. For a time, perhaps for many years, your soul will shrivel in the fire of God's wrath. The time can be shortened if somebody will have masses read for your soul. I will read masses if I am paid for them, otherwise you will have to take your medicine." I would hate to think of dying with somebody like that at my bedside. To the other comes a Lutheran pastor. He brings with him the Bible. From it he gives the assurance that for the dying Christian the time of all suffering is now at an end. From the Word of God he reads to him, "Blessed are the dead which die in the Lord from henceforth," from now on, as soon as you close your eyes. "Verily, verily I say unto thee, to-day shalt thou be with me in paradise." "Where sin abounds, there doth grace much more abound." "There remaineth, therefore, no condemnation to them that are in Christ Jesus." You belong to the Lutheran Church. Thank God for it. For you death is not a torture chamber. It is a release, an entrance to eternal life.

Reformation Day, however, is not only an appropriate time to take stock, to take inventory of the blessings that have come to us through our citizenship in the United States, and through our membership in the Lutheran Church, but it is a challenge to dedicate ourselves anew to the preservation of our civil and religious liberty.

Once freedom is lost it can be won back only at a terrible price. In that cold winter of 1777 the soldiers of George Washington wrote the price of liberty on the snow of Valley Forge with the blood that oozed from their frostbitten feet. Martin Luther, kneeling in agony in his monk's cell and wrestling with God in prayer; Gustavus Adolphus, sinking to the ground in the battle of Luetzen; Christ in Gethsemane lifting His bloodsmeared face to heaven and pleading for the cup of suffering to be removed — these are the pages on which the price of regaining lost freedom is written down.

This is not a time to feel secure in our freedom. It may be that right now we are standing at the crossroads. Ever since the shooting war has ended, Russia's communism and our American way of life, like two prizefighters in the opening round, have been feinting and sparring for time, feeling each other out, looking for vulnerability. When will the first blow fall? We know that communism has its agents right here in our land. Twenty years ago it would have been difficult to find a handful of men willing to confess that they were communists. Today there are 20,000 registered communists. Who knows how many more there are? Communism has its dupes among men of high station, aspiring to leadership. Do not tell me that they are sincere. Maybe they are. The sincerity of a fool only makes his foolishness more dangerous. Nothing can please our enemies more than to hear Americans say, "It can't happen over here." It can and it will if we are not on guard. Let us thank God that right now we are the most powerful nation on earth. But let us not forget that every other world power was sooner or later overcome, impossible as that seemed in the day of greatness. God wants to see us on our knees, praying for peace and good government, even as Christ spent a great deal of time on His knees, and as Luther did. But He also wants to see us on our feet. Having knelt in the Garden of Gethsemane, Christ said, "Arise, let us go!" In Worms Luther spent the night in prayer, but he also stood before the emperor and the dignitaries of state and church with his defiant, "Unless I am convinced by clear passages of Holy Writ, I will recant nothing. Here I stand, I cannot do otherwise, God help me! Amen." We should pray; we should vote, even if it be only for the lesser of two evils; but we should also personally work for good government and for the preservation of freedom. The men and women of our church to whom God has given the blessings of education, of political understanding, the gift of speech, and the power of the pen — they owe it to themselves, and to their children, and to their country, and to their church, and to God, to seek office and leadership, in order that righteousness may exalt the nation.

You cannot surrender civil freedom without sacrificing religious liberty as well. Ask the millions of Russians who were not only driven out of their homes, but out of their churches as well.

We sing, "Like a mighty army moves the Church of God." This is not always true. But it can be true; a church, first on its knees, and then on its feet; a church praying Christ to lead on, and ready to follow into battle, cannot be conquered.

At the entrance to our Druid Hill Park in my own city of Baltimore one sees a great statue of Luther, not in the pose of the protesting Luther of Worms, but in the pose of the preaching Luther of America, right arm raised to heaven, left arm holding the Book to his side and to his heart. Luther did much for the Book. He translated it; he put it back in the hands of the people; he enthroned it as the only authority in the church. But the Book also did much for him. It led him out of the darkness into the light, out of spiritual ignorance to spiritual knowledge. Through it, he who had groveled before Christ as a slave before his taskmaster, stood before Christ, his Saviour, as a liberated child of God. It drew him away from the brink of despair to a glorious hope. It was to him the sword of the spirit, the weapon of truth that made him mighty in battle.

Thus I would have the world see the Lutheran Church, with the Bible pressed to the heart, with the hand upraised in the preaching of the Gospel of Christ, as she defiantly, but also gratefully, cries out, "God's Word and Luther's doctrine pure to all eternity shall endure." *Amen.*

# 33

## *Inner Thankfulness*

### (Thanksgiving)
II Thessalonians 2:13

*But we are bound to give thanks alway to God for you, brethren beloved of the Lord, because God hath from the beginning chosen you to salvation through sanctification of the Spirit and belief of the truth:*

Our Thanksgiving Day is as American as anything can be. It is as American as the turkey which graces our table today. It grew out of the thankfulness of settlers for the new way of life which lay before them in their new country.

The Pilgrims, when they planned the first American Thanksgiving Day, were not only thankful for what they had, but also for what they hoped to have. When they saw how lavishly the virgin soil of their acres responded to their tilling and sowing, they no longer merely hoped, but assured one another that hunger and starvation need no longer be feared. For what they had and hoped to have they were deeply grateful. In the words of our text: They were "bound to give thanks."

Thankful as they were, the happy Pilgrims could not — could not by the widest stretch of their imagination — have foreseen what was to come from the humble beginning they had made. The wild turkey, which they knew and which they hunted for their Thanksgiving dinner, has been domesticated, and multiplied and multiplied, so that in these several weeks thousands of trucks, and many trains and ships have carried turkeys to Americans everywhere. The few ears of corn, which they laid away for seed, have multiplied and multiplied, so that towering elevators cannot contain the crop. The miracle of the loaves and fishes is repeated in the miracle of the corn and the turkey. They symbolize the growth and prosperity of America.

Today, grateful Americans raise their voices in their churches in a great anthem of thanksgiving. And this afternoon and evening families and friends will gather around laden tables, and there will be merrymaking everywhere. And this is not only American, but Biblical.

When, after the long Babylonian captivity, the people of Israel were returned to their own country and when the rebuilding of the temple was finished, they, too, held a Thanksgiving Day. In the morning they met for a great national service of worship and praise. And then, when they had voiced their gratitude to God, Ezra and Nehemiah said unto them, "Go your way, eat the fat, and drink the sweet, and send portions to them for whom nothing is prepared: for this day is holy unto the LORD."

Says the Apostle, "We are bound to give thanks alway to God." These words of the Bible are directed to all people of the world and apply to all people everywhere. All mankind is "bound to give thanks alway to God." But, surely, we Americans must admit that this is a directive to us, coming with far greater force to us than to many others.

Thanksgiving days should couple certain words in our American minds and link them together — words like "thinking" and "thanking"; "getting" and "giving." A glance into the concordance of your Bible will suffice to show that the words "thanksgiving" and "thinking" are found in just about an equal number of times on the pages of Holy Writ.

Only a thinking person can be truly thankful. This becomes all the more apparent when we are mindful of the fact that we should be thankful not only for material gifts, but also for spiritual blessings. Perhaps it is natural for us to think first of material gifts; all the more because this is a national holiday and a harvest festival. And when it comes to material possessions, we Americans are the envy of the world. The first winter brought famine for the pilgrims. But that was the last famine our people ever suffered. What a country — when one of our everyday problems is to find a parking place for our automobile. We Americans are so rich that we cannot be envious of the people of other nations; we can only be envious of other Americans. Our federal agents are constantly hard pressed to prevent the smuggling of aliens into our country. Only recently we read the caption in the newspapers, "Smugglers take to the air." By airplane, they are smuggled in from Cuba, Mexico, and elsewhere. The established fare is from $700 to $1000 per head. So eager are people to come here. Other countries do not have that problem, at least not as far as Americans are concerned. Who wants to leave America? The waiting list of those seeking to enter our country legally runs into the thousands. Surely, a little pondering of the Apostle's word, "We are bound to give thanks to God alway," should strike a chord of agreement in our hearts.

A little deeper thinking will make us doubly grateful for our spiritual blessings. Why are others not only ready but eager to sever the ties which bind them to their homeland and to come here? They are not moved merely by the desire to own an automobile, or by the desire for a better-paying job, or by the hope of a home with gas heat and running water; no, it is American freedom for which they long. We have never experienced such longing because with our first breath we inhaled the air of freedom. Foreigners tell us we can have no understanding of the nervous tension associated with the constant fear that one is being watched and spied on. One thoughtless word often means the concentration camp or exile to distant parts. It is horrible to have your entire life so ordered by government that you cannot call your soul your own. Always there is the torturous insecurity of not knowing what the next day may bring.

We hear much these days of Formosa and of the often-shelled Quemoy. Thousands of Chinese live there who fled from the mainland to escape the terrors of communism. They left their homes and occupations and factories and shops. Most of them still have dear ones who remained behind. Homesickness gnaws at their hearts. They know it would spell the end if the communists should overrun them. We know not, thank God, what it means to live under such conditions.

Yes, the spiritual blessings we enjoy far outweigh any material advantage we have over others. For our freedom, for our liberty, "we are bound alway to give thanks to God." Paul once wrote a sentence to the Philippians which should strongly appeal to us. He wrote, "whatsoever things are true, whatsoever things are honest, whatsoever things are just, whatsoever things are pure, whatsoever things are of good report; if there be any virtue, and if there be any praise, think on these things." "Think on these things." These things in the end mean far more than gold or silver, or any other material riches. Think! You will be the more ready to thank.

However, there is another thought which should not elude our thinking today — two words which should be linked together; namely, "receive" and "giving." There are two sentences which we know Christ spoke, which are not recorded in any of the four Gospels. We owe it to Paul that these words are not lost to us. One reads, "It is more blessed to give than to receive." Receiving is good, but giving is better. A good giver is better than a good taker. We are all givers and takers. We daily take from God, and we should be good takers, good receivers, not only when His gifts come in the frame of joy but also when they come in the frame of sorrow. The Psalmist says, "I will take the cup of salvation, and call upon the name of the Lord." Every Christian has his own individual cup of salvation. And God knows exactly how to mix its ingredients, so many spoonfuls of joy, so many drops of sorrow. The Psalmist says, "Whatever God puts into my cup I will drink, and call upon his name," that is, ask Him for more. The Christian always proves his Christianity by the manner in which he takes what God gives.

God promised the children of Israel that He would deliver

them from the slavery of Egypt and lead them to the promised land. He promised every individual in Israel that he should sit under his own vine and under his own fig tree. And the children of Israel took their deliverance from God. But how? Not with thanksgiving, but rather with constant murmuring and grumbling. There are so many thankless people because there are so many poor takers, poor receivers.

God gives us so much that He is called the "Giver." He is the "Giver of all good gifts." It follows that we, His children, should also be givers of good gifts. That is what Nehemiah had in mind when he told the children of Israel, on their Thanksgiving Day, "Take portions to them for whom nothing is prepared."

The Christian gives without being told. It is natural and instinctive for him to give; for thus alone can he show his gratitude to God. When Christian congregations on this day lift a thank offering, it is not to exploit the opportunity, but to give their members an outlet for the spirit of giving.

This is a national holiday. Today we think first of all as Americans. In the consciousness that we are the most blessed people on earth, we realize that we ought to share our blessings with other, less fortunate nations. One thing is certainly true; we have been giving, not in thousands, or millions, but in billions. But, how much of it is blessed giving? I am not criticizing the government for contributing huge sums to other nations to assist them in arming against the encroachments of communism. Nevertheless, if we had given one-fourth as much for mission work and for the charity which always goes with it, would the threat of communism haunt us now, as it does? Communism grows out of the poverty, and despair, and hopelessness of people. Mission work must now of necessity be carried on by Americans; for some nations formerly active in mission work are now mission fields.

Needless to say to you, our thinking and thanking, our giving and getting, must be sanctified by love for our Saviour Jesus Christ. Once, after He had healed a group of ten lepers, He was bitterly disappointed when only one returned to give thanks. How much greater His disappointment if those whom He healed from the leprosy of sin are not thankful. He is the

Benefactor. When we were enslaved by sin, He set us free. He purchased and won us with a price which must forever stagger our imagination. We were the chattels of Satan, but God made us His children and heirs of salvation. Today we pray for world peace, while thanking our Saviour for filling our hearts with peace beyond understanding. For us every day is a thanksgiving day. May the Holy Spirit make us better Americans by making us better Christians; may He bless our land as He has so richly blessed it in the past; and may He bless us and make us a blessing to others, by holding out to them the peace which Christ offers to all who are weak and heavy laden. *Amen.*

# 34

## Mission Work Under Difficulties

### (Missions)
### Jeremiah 1:19

*And they shall fight against thee; but they shall not prevail against thee; for I am with thee, saith the LORD, to deliver thee.*

The aim of all mission endeavor is the salvation of souls. These days that almost sounds ridiculous. If we close our eyes to the Word of God and consult only our own hearts and minds, we see little incentive for missionary activity. The minds of men are turned to the destruction of human lives rather than to the salvation of souls. As always, there are shooting wars, but they unsettle the routine existence of man far less than the cold war. As our Secretary of State shuttles back and forth across the Atlantic, hastening from conference to conference, our inventors spend sleepless nights, our engineers seek to translate theory into practice, our government strives to aid freedom-loving democracies and to curb others, who are seeking large loans for their own selfish ends. Almost our entire electronics industry is geared to manufacture ever more deadly and destructive instruments of war. To get there first with the most destructive force, that is the crying need.

Kill! kill! kill! Why speak of saving souls? It is like a horror movie, whose producer and director is Satan, himself.

It must fill Satan with hellish glee when he sees how heavily Christians are contributing to the destruction of human lives. When you drink a cup of tea, when you buy a loaf of bread, when you purchase a yard of cloth, when you pay your admission to some sport or entertainment (for all of which you are taxed), you are contributing for the manufacture of deadly weapons of some kind. As often as you sign a legal document, as often as you order the sale or purchase of a bond or a share of stock, you are helping to pay for a bomber, or submarine, or missile. Ironically, every Christian in the world is contributing to the destruction of human lives. They are contributing millions. What they give for missions is insignificant by comparison.

If Christians had contributed one half of the amount for missions which they now contribute for war preparation, if they had taxed themselves one half of the amount for the Lord's work which they now are taxed for Satan's work, would there be so great a threat of war? We have reason to hang our heads in shame; we have reason to repent; we should acknowledge that by our negligence we are responsible for the deplorable human relationships existing today. Is it too late? Have the forces of evil conquered the kingdom of God?

Listen to the words of the text: "They shall fight against thee; but they shall not prevail against thee; for I am with thee, saith the LORD, to deliver thee." God spoke these words to His young prophet, Jeremiah. And this promise was made in a day when social conditions were, if anything, worse than they are now. Time does not permit a detailed account of life in Israel and in the world at that time. Never were people more highly favored, more contemptuously ungrateful, and more severely punished than were the Jews. And in his day, Jeremiah was their prophet. They hounded and persecuted him. In a bedlam of idolatrous voices, his call to repentance went unheeded. Instead of imprisonment, he could have enjoyed a life of ease and plenty by going over to the enemy of Israel as an appeaser. But, though his people spurned him, he chose to share their lot.

God had promised that salvation should come out of Israel. At the time, however, it seemed that Israel was accursed, and could only become a curse to others. Judged by human thinking, it was no time for missionary undertaking. Yes, it seemed utterly ridiculous for one prophet, hardly more than a lad, to fight the Lord's battle single-handed. However, his faith in the promise of the Lord encouraged Jeremiah to believe that salvation would yet come out of Israel. Above all, he was mightily strengthened by the promise given to him personally, "They shall fight against thee, but they shall not prevail." And in the end his confidence was justified, when after the long Babylonian captivity, true worship was revived in Israel. The final vindication of his faith, and that of all other prophets of Israel, came when the Gospel of the death and resurrection of Christ went out from Israel into all the world. Tremendous opposition was only a greater challenge to Jeremiah to do his utmost and to trust in God, leaving the fulfillment of all promises to Him.

Opposition and difficulties have never frightened the missionaries of Christ when they believed His promises. From Ephesus, Paul once wrote a letter to the Corinthians, telling them how eager he was to visit them but that he felt constrained to remain longer in Ephesus. "There are many adversaries," he wrote. They did not frighten him. He did not remain despite them, but because of them. One could hardly think of a less fertile mission field than Ephesus. The presence of the "many adversaries" was a challenge to Paul to fight and win.

My friends, this is no time for Christians to hang their heads and to speak of hopeless prospects. God still lives. Even now we see God's hand in the turn of events. Hitler was determined to dethrone the God of heaven and to enthrone a god with Nordic blood in his veins. Our government sent arms and ammunition to Stalin, who was fighting Hitler, but who was also fighting against God and who sought to root out Christianity in Russia altogether. Christians were bewildered. Long ago Christ had spoken of the folly of trying to drive out devils by devils. Lutherans were shocked by the murder of hundreds of pastors by Hitler as well as Stalin. Christians were dismayed when they heard how successfully and how easily dictators had turned the hearts of their nations against God. Now we have learned not to believe dictators; now we know how greatly those reports were exaggerated. Hitler is dead and his Nordic god went down into the gasoline-drenched pit with him. The Gospel is still preached in Germany. Stalin is dead, but God still lives in Russia. In the Easter season we read of crowded churches in Moscow.

The Reds in China were not deterred by the failure of Hitler and Stalin to depose God. They also declared war against Him. However, today Chinese are flocking into Christian churches in Formosa and Hongchow. And we may be sure that on the mainland of China many converts remain true to their Saviour, though now they may be as silent as the seven thousand were in Elijah's day.

The war, which many predicted would be the end of the Christian Church, opened up many new fields, which are now white unto the harvest — such as Japan, New Guinea, and other countries, hitherto untouched by the Gospel.

We do not know what God has in mind; we do not know what new doors He will open to missionaries; but we do know there will always be open doors, for He said, "I have set before thee an open door and no man shall shut it." The important thing is that we be ready to enter through whatever doors God may open before us.

As has been pointed out, we are all contributing to the destruction of human lives. We have no choice. But will God excuse us if we do not offset these involuntary contributions to Satan's work by even greater voluntary contributions to the great work of the Lord? Only Christianity has a constructive program. What is the world fighting for? Communists claim they are fighting for a new order, which will save the world. We say, if that order is established it will ruin the world. Christ also wants a new order, a new order that can put a stop to strife, war, and hatred. He says, "If ye continue in my word, then ye shall be my disciples indeed, and ye shall know the truth, and the truth shall make you free." Only when men are united in Christ are they free from strife and hatred. That is an end worth working for. By that program we are not merely working for a better world, but for the eternal salvation of souls. Now, more than ever, we must obey our Lord's great command to preach the Gospel to every creature.

We, too, have the promise, "They shall fight against thee; but they shall not prevail against thee: for I am with thee, saith the Lord, to deliver thee." His promise has never failed. Think how this promise was fulfilled in our Saviour. Oh, they fought against Him. They fought against Him from babyhood through manhood. It began when Herod ordered the murder of the babes of Bethlehem, hoping to nip His mission in the bud. It never ended. Even when He was dead, they placed soldiers around His grave to keep Him there. They tried to hurl Him from a cliff in Nazareth; they tried to stone Him; they tried to arouse the suspicion of the Roman government; they tried to entangle Him in His own words. Again and again, Satan tempted Him. Says the Psalmist, "He that sitteth in the heavens shall laugh." They fought against Him but they could not prevail against Him. And we have His promise that the portals of hell shall not prevail against us.

Mission work should be a joy. When we have something which costs us nothing, should we not be willing to share it with others? Our salvation cost us nothing. It cost Him His life. We could do nothing. We were hopelessly lost in sin. We did not love Him, He loved us. He atoned for all our sins by His bitter suffering and death. He suffered for all others also. But many do not know that. It is for us to tell them. It is for us to bring to others the peace and happiness in Him which fills our own hearts. If you love Him, you will let nothing stop you. *Amen.*

# 35

## *Abounding Grace*

(Anniversary)
Hebrews 2:6-8

*But one in a certain place testified, saying, What is man, that thou art mindful of him? or the son of man, that thou visitest him? Thou madest him a little lower than the angels; thou crownedst him with glory and honour, and didst set him over the works of thy hands: Thou hast put all things in subjection under his feet. For in that he put all in subjection under him, he left nothing that is not put under him. But now we see not yet all things put under him.*

(This sermon was preached in Richmond, Va., in the year 1952, when the Southeastern District of the Lutheran Church, Missouri Synod, met in convention in Bethlehem Church, which in that year celebrated its one hundredth anniversary.)

The writer of the Epistle to the Hebrews introduces this text with the words, "One in a certain place testified." It is a manner of speech with which we are quite familiar. We too say, "Someone has said," or, "It has been said," or, "It is written."

In this instance, however, we know who the "one" is whom the Apostle here quotes. It was David, in the eighth psalm.

187

He was doing what we so greatly enjoy doing — he was standing in the night gazing at the moon and the stars. He was overwhelmed by the heavenly beauty.

The surface of our earth measures one hundred and ninety million square miles. And David knew what a tiny, little orbit it is in limitless space. Uranus is eighty times greater than the earth; Saturn is nine hundred and ninety-five times greater; and Jupiter is one thousand, two hundred and eighty-one times greater. David did not mention the sun; for it was night, of course. Yet, if we can believe astronomers, other planets in other galaxies are far larger than our sun.

There stood David in the night and told himself, "God made it all, this unbelievable universe, whose vastness no one will ever fully comprehend." Nor did it tax His strength. David said, "When I consider the work of thy fingers." What fingers! and then, in introspection and self-appraisal, he admitted, "Surely, compared to the whole of creation, I stand here as an infinitesimal speck, smaller than a grain of sand on the seashore." As if ashamed for even thinking of himself, he asks, "What is man that thou are mindful of him?" Yes, what is man and what are all men together that God should give them a second thought?

Nevertheless, in His Son Christ Jesus God "visited man." In the beginning God made man second in rank only to the angels. He gave him dominion over all the earth. He "crowned him with glory and honor." Man forfeited his lofty station when he fell into sin. Then the unbelievable, the altogether unexpected happened — in His love God redeemed fallen man. To that end He made His own Son "a little lower than the angels . . . that he by the grace of God should taste death for every man."

Christ did taste death for every man. It was customary in ancient times to take off criminals by compelling them to drink a cup of poison. Thus the Athenian magistrates ordered Socrates to drink a cup of hemlock juice. The sentence was one of the most unjust ever pronounced on any man. Socrates was not only innocent of crime, but at the time most certainly the greatest benefactor of his country. When the poison was brought to him, his friends begged him to put off drinking it as long as possible; but he would not. He took it cheerfully and drank it with alacrity.

The writer of the text sees the entire human race judged, condemned, and sentenced to drink the cup of poison concocted by its own sin. But Jesus, as it were, took the cup of death from the hand of every man and drank it for him.

Socrates was innocent of the crime with which he was charged. Nevertheless, he was a sinner and, therefore, mortal. He knew, now or a little later, it could make little difference. But Jesus was not a sinner. Hence, He was not mortal. His death was not the unavoidable consequence of some sin of His own. His death came "by the grace of God." The death of Christ was the greatest manifestation of God's grace.

Again we ask, "What is man that thou art mindful of him?" In consequence of Adam's sin the whole human race became sinful in its nature, and, in practice, added transgression to sinfulness of disposition, thus becoming exposed to endless perdition. Now, what was man?

God had made the first Adam only a little lower than the angels. What a striking, wonderful couple our first parents must have been! When Adam looked at his Eve he must have exclaimed, as Solomon did in his song, "How fair and how pleasant art thou, O love!" Adam, too, could speak of the work of his fingers. God gave him a hand with which to fashion wonders, and a mind so nimble that it feared no problems. And God gave man a will, like His own, to do what was right and good.

Oh, what a wreck that noble creature became when the serpent's poison coursed through his veins! Look at him now! Look at him as the inspired prophet Isaiah sees him — "The whole head is sick, and the whole heart is faint. From the sole of the foot even unto the head there is no soundness in it, but wounds, and bruises, and putrifying sores."

And yet, God did not turn away from that ugly sight with loathing. Instead He said, I must start all over again. However, this time it was not so easy; this time it was not merely a task for His fingers. This time the Triune God had to go into council with Himself. He had to probe to the very depths of His divine wisdom to devise a plan of salvation. God asked

His Son to volunteer for a mission of horrors, which would mean the hunting down of the hellish serpent, to crush its head. God told His Son the plan necessitated a sojourn, extended over the life of one human generation, in the filthy world below, in the company of sinners. He told Him, You will have to do what they are unable to do for themselves; You will have to fulfill the law for them by leading a holy, spotless life under never-ending temptations. And, finally, You will have to bear the punishment for their sins; You will have to die a horrible death in their stead. Of this the Apostle was thinking when he said, "That he by the grace of God should taste death for every man."

Was there anything, whatever, in man that could move God to expend such grace upon him? God never looks for goodness in any man. It would be like looking for grapes on thorns, or for figs on thistles. Man's heart is like a poisoned spring emitting the reeking vapors of evil thoughts, words, and deeds. No, God does not look for good in any man. He knows better. But, God imputes goodness. God saved us, not because we were good, but because He is good. In holy baptism we put on the goodness of Christ — we put it on as a garment to hide our sinfulness. It is all grace, incomprehensible, divine, perfect grace. "By the grace of God Christ tasted death for every man."

For this grace of God we should give thanks without ceasing. There came a day when David was so impressed with the fulness of God's grace that his heart burst forth in the poetic exultation: "Bless the Lord, O my soul, and all that is within me, bless his holy name. Bless the Lord, O my soul, and forget not all his benefits; who forgiveth all thine iniquities; who healeth all thy diseases; who redeemeth thy life from destruction; who crowneth thee with lovingkindness and tender mercies." Such must be the thoughts of our hearts also, every day, without exception.

God's grace comes not as a single gift, bestowed once; no, God's grace comes like a steady and constant stream. He is "the God of grace." The Apostle speaks of "the exceeding riches of his grace." We are invited "boldly to come to the throne of grace." The Bible calls us "heirs of grace."

This evening our hearts are stirred by a twofold recollection of God's grace. We think of the blessings which He bestowed upon our Southeastern District since its inception, and we think of His marvelous grace given to this congregation in the century of its existence.

When you, the members of Bethlehem, invited Synod to meet here and to celebrate your one hundredth anniversary with you, you followed in the footsteps of your fathers. When they, in the year 1868, dedicated the new church, in which you were domiciled until this edifice was erected, they also invited Synod to meet here in Richmond, to rejoice with them.

A retrospect to that convention must strike in our hearts a chord of deep appreciation for the grace which God shed upon Synod and upon this congregation. It was a memorable convention for my own congregation, Martini, of Baltimore; for it was in 1868 that Martini Church was dedicated, and it was here in Richmond that Martini was received into membership by Synod.

The President of the Eastern District, Pastor Keyl, opened the convention of 1868 with an invitation to join him in the praises of the Almighty whose grace had granted phenomenal growth to Synod during the twenty-two years of its existence.

The President of the Missouri Synod, Dr. Walther, whose post-office address is recorded in the report of that year as Concordia University, St. Louis, Mo., preached the convention sermon. His text was I Cor. 3:11-15 — "Other foundation can no man lay than that is laid, which is Jesus Christ." He was also the essayist of the convention. His theme was, "The Lutheran Church assigns to every doctrine of God's Word the position and significance which the Bible, itself, assigns to it." In his unique and masterful way, under twelve subdivisions, he pointed out how the Christian must distinguish between the doctrines of Scripture. "Some," he said, "are the very foundation of the entire structure; some are built on the foundation; some furnish the roof; while others are of a decorative character. But all, fundamental or non-fundamental, are the Word of God, and accepted as such by the Lutheran Church."

One important item of business entailed lengthy discussion; namely, the creation of a publishing establishment. Both the Northern and the Eastern Districts of Synod had submitted memorials to the general body advocating the venture. The convention now implemented its petition with seven weighty and convincing arguments. The fruition of the petition came with the founding of Concordia Publishing House in the following year, 1869.

The treasurer's report revealed a total income of $3,812 for the Eastern District, and disbursements of $3,716. This was a source of satisfaction. At this convention it was reported yesterday that the income of our little Southeastern District for the past year was $275,000. This does not include the $150,000 which the district gathered in the "Conquest for Christ." Those delegates to the 1868 convention never dreamed of a day when the districts of Synod would collect for the Lord's cause $15,000,000 in a single year.

In the year 1868 the Eastern District of Synod boasted of 38 pastors. Now we have more than 250 in the same area. Then they were planning a publishing concern. The dream not only became a reality, but Concordia Publishing House is now the largest Lutheran publishing establishment in the world.

However, material progress would be meaningless if in the intervening years the one pearl of great price had been lost. I am speaking of the pure doctrine of God's holy Word, and of the faith in it. Thank God, that did not happen. At the convention in 1868 the President of the Missouri Synod was present; his successor is present at this convention. And he is speaking the same language. The sermon of Dr. Behnken on Monday evening was but the echo of Dr. Walther's sermon, preached here eighty-four years ago. Both stressed the fact that loyalty to God's Word is our most important business.

You, the members of Bethlehem, shared in the outpouring of God's grace. This congregation was organized in the year 1852. Sixteen years later your fathers built their new church, which still serves as a house of worship for another congregation. One wonders where they found courage to build so soon after the war between the States, which had caused such havoc here in Richmond. They incurred what under the circumstances must have been a staggering debt. In the report of the convention of 1868 I read, "The President urged the congregations of the district to come to the assistance of the small group of people, who suffered so greatly during the terrible war, and who have already accomplished the seemingly impossible."

The cost of the church then was $11,000. Today your annual income is considerably larger. For the recent "Conquest for Christ collection" the offering of your congregation exceeded the income of the entire Eastern District of that day. You not only replaced your former house of worship with this beautiful edifice, but you liberally assisted your daughter congregation in the building of the church which was recently dedicated.

God not only gave you able pastors, but He gave them grace never to depart from the preaching of the glorious Gospel of Christ. It is inspiring to think that today your parents and grandparents, as saints above, still form one communion with you, while the Lord, before whose throne they stand, still sees here a green pasture, where His sheep and His lambs are nourished beside still waters with the one food that can satisfy the soul.

In the name of the delegates here assembled I thank you for the cordial hospitality afforded us this week, and especially, for the opportunity to rejoice with you over the grace of God, which He bestowed upon you.

And now, may He who tasted death for all men, and for you, bless you, and keep you, and give you grace to continue working with Him in the building of His great kingdom. *Amen.*

# 36

## *When God Ordains*

### (Ordination)
### Jeremiah 1:5-8

*Before I formed thee in the belly I knew thee; and before thou camest forth out of the womb I sanctified thee, and I ordained thee a prophet unto the nations. Then said I, Ah, Lord GOD! behold, I cannot speak: for I am a child. But the LORD said unto me, Say not, I am a child: for thou shalt go to all that I shall send thee, and whatsoever I command thee thou shalt speak. Be not afraid of their faces: for I am with thee to deliver thee, saith the LORD.*

No true servant of the Lord has ever been called into the ministry without fear and trembling.

When God ordained Moses and instructed him to proceed to Egypt with the demand upon Pharaoh to permit the children of Israel to emigrate from Egypt to the Promised Land, Moses was afraid. He did not fear recognition as a former member of the royal household, or as the killer of an Egyptian overseer. Forty years had erased much of the memory of his former life in Egypt. He did not fear for his life. He feared failure. He was conscious of his own inadequacy for so great a mission. He hemmed and hawed and dodged about. He offered all manner of excuses — the people would not heed him — he was not a ready speaker — his tongue was heavy.

194

Finally he refused outright. "Send," he said, "I pray thee, by the hand of him whom thou wilt send." God had to compel him to go.

We observe the same reluctance in Jonah, who certainly was not a timid or cowardly man. Why was he fleeing, taking a ship westward for Tarshish instead of a camel eastward to Nineveh? When the ship was caught in a storm, the superstitious sailors cast lots to determine who was the cause of this evil. When the lot fell upon Jonah, the sailors faced a new dilemma. They hestitated to lay hands on a prophet of God. So they asked him, "What shall we do unto thee, that the sea may be calm?" "Pitch me into the sea," he said. That was not the answer of a coward. Yet he fled when God told him to go to Nineveh, there to preach repentance. He preferred to walk into the jaws of death, rather than through the gates of Nineveh. Why? Because he feared failure; because he felt he was not the man for the task; because he feared the mighty men of Nineveh would laugh him to scorn.

And so it was with Jeremiah. When God informed him that He had ordained him as a prophet to the nations, Jeremiah was afraid. He said, "Ah, Lord GOD! behold, I cannot speak: for I am a child." Luther's translation renders it, *"Ich bin zu jung."* "I am too young." He meant to say, "I am scarcely more than a boy; I am wholly inexperienced; I am utterly incapable of couching divine truths in adequate language; I will be ignored, completely lacking all appearance of authority."

Always, the true servant of the Lord, when called into the ministry, feels his own unworthiness and ineptitude. He knows the awful responsibility that attaches to the ministry, and nothing but the call of God can induce him to undertake it. On the other hand, those who have no divine call have no such feeling of awesomeness. They are fearless, brazen, and arrogant. They have the temerity to run hither and yon. They arbitrarily burden men with laws and ordinances of which God is not the author. Says the poet:

> *How ready is the man to go,*
> *Whom God hath never sent!*

*How timorous, diffident, and slow*
*God's chosen instrument.*

I doubt not, dear brother, that this hour arouses kindred thoughts in your heart also. Uppermost, perhaps, is the thought of your unworthiness to assume the office of the ministry. You are to warn others against sin and condemn sin in their lives, while you, yourself, are a sinner. You are to announce absolution to others, and are in need of it yourself. You are to be an ambassador of Christ, before whose shining countenance the angels shield their faces, though like John the Baptist, you know that you are not worthy to unloose His shoes' latchets. This sense of unfitness is ever with older pastors also. It stems in part from inner convictions, and in part from the jeers of Satan, who would rob them of joy and confidence in their calling by flaunting their imperfections before their faces.

Then, too, there is the thought of your youth. You are to teach older people, who are far your seniors in the school of experience. In the sickroom you are to give a better understanding of life to some who have lived a lifetime. In the congregational meetings you are to demand the respect of men who hold lofty positions in the social, business, and political world. You are aware that neither polished manners nor clerical dress can hide your youth and inexperience.

Finally, you are troubled by the lack of precedent. In dealing with men and their problems you will be confronted by situations with which you have not met before. You will be forced by circumstances to make decisions, and right decisions.

I doubt not that in this hour you are inclined, like Moses, to balk. Once I heard one of my teachers, a highly respected doctor of theology, say that he balked all his life; that God had to compel him to accept every new call to a more responsible office. I doubt not that, like Jonah, you would like to run away from it all. I doubt not that like Jeremiah, you feel inclined to protest, "Ah, Lord GOD! behold, I cannot speak: for I am a child."

Nor would I have you feel otherwise. The candidate for the ministry, who despairs of his own powers but trusts in God's help, is far better equipped than he who considers himself peculiarly well qualified.

However, you must not let unworthiness, youth, and lack of experience rob you of the joy of this day. God's answer to Jeremiah was, "I am with thee." That is a most comforting assurance. Today God is clothing you with authority, with authority to speak for Him. And, when you exercise this authority, He pledges Himself to stand back of you. Think what this means. Lately there have been many international conferences, and so-called peace conferences. Our delegates have told the representatives of other nations, "We seek friendly relationships and peace. We want to assist you in stabilizing your national economy. We offer you good will and fair trade treaties. We will do all this if you let us. But if any nation rises up against us or tyrannizes any of our fellow-democratic friends, we will destroy that nation." Now, our national delegate is only one man. Nevertheless he can speak as he does because he is clothed with authority, because back of him stands the richest and mightiest nation of all the world. But, back of you stands Almighty God, who has vested you with authority. You can say to men, "I offer you God's friendship, good will, and eternal peace. I will show you the way to eternal life, if you let me; but I will remand you to God's eternal judgment if you compel me."

"I am with thee." Today He gives you this promise. What need you fear? Being with you, He will give you the wisdom to say and do what any situation demands, inexperienced as you may be. If He is with you, He will clothe you with dignity in the sight of men, despite your youth. God knows no failure. However weak the instrument, He accomplishes by it that which pleases Him. What He begins He brings to glorious completion. The balking Moses, the fleeing Jonah, the stammering Jeremiah became great, because God accomplished great things through them.

However, to become partaker of their blessings you must, as they were in the end, truly be a spokeman of the Lord. To Jeremiah God said, "Behold, I have put my words in thy mouth." The minister's business is to preach the Word of God. If I feared that you would ever preach anything but the

Word of God, I would ask you to walk away now from the altar of the Lord, before making your vow of ordination. God is still against the prophets "who use their tongue and say, God saith."

What the world today needs as much as ever is the preaching of God's Word. Sinful man's life in this world is of short duration — soon he goes, either to heaven, or to hell; either to joy such "as eye hath not seen and ear hath not heard," or to unthinkable torture. What could be more important than to teach men to believe right and to live right, so that they may die right? This is what you can do, and this is what you must do. To do otherwise would debauch your entire ministry. You are dealing with immortal souls, and there is only one Saviour of souls.

Men have sacrificed millions of sheep and oxen. Some have sacrificed their sons and daughters; and others have castigated and mutilated their own bodies and shed their own blood. Their sacrifices were a stench in the nostrils of God. Says the psalmist, "None of them can by any means redeem his brother, nor give to God a ransom for him." To redeem, to buy back, is a prerogative reserved entirely to one who first possesssed what is to be redeemed. God made us. We were His. Only He could redeem us. And He did.

It required the greatest possible sacrifice. That sacrifice was made when Christ laid aside His heavenly majesty and abode on this sinful earth as a servant, and as the Servant of servants. His holy life, His perfect obedience to the law of God, was a lifelong sacrifice offered to His Father in atonement for our wicked lives. His agony in Gethsemane and on the cross was a punishment for our sins. It was the supreme, but also the perfect sacrifice. It was voluntary. No sheep and no ox ever was a willing sacrifice, nor was any human being. Life was taken from them. Christ laid down His life. He died because He wanted to die, and He died when He wanted to die; because there was no other way to save men from death.

All His merit is wrapped up in the Gospel and in the Sacrament. In them, and in them alone, is healing power for sin-sick mankind. Preach the Gospel to every creature — he that believeth shall be saved.

Accompanied by the promise of God that He will be with you is another divine promise; namely, that you will not preach the Gospel in vain. It will do its work as the rain and the snow do their work. If you will preach the Gospel to the exclusion of all else, you are divinely assured that on the day of resurrection men will stand before the throne of God, and will point to you, and say, "There stands the man who led us to this blessed goal. Thanks and praise be to Thee, O God, for having put Thy word in his mouth." Will that be reward enough for you? If so, preach "Christ and Him crucified." *Amen.*

# 37

## Dead Wood in the Church

(Installation)
Ezekiel 15:1-5

*And the word of the LORD came unto me, saying, Son of man, What is the vine tree more than any tree, or than a branch which is among the trees of the forest? Shall wood be taken thereof to do any work? or will men take a pin of it to hang any vessel thereon? Behold, it is cast into the fire for fuel; the fire devoureth both the ends of it, and the midst of it is burned. Is it meet for any work? Behold, when it was whole, it was meet for no work: how much less shall it be meet yet for any work, when the fire hath devoured it and it is burned?*

Wherever the internal affairs of the church are discussed, complaint is voiced that there is much dead wood. The principal function of wood is the transporting of water and salt, drawn from the soil by the roots, to the leaves and fruit of the tree. Dead wood transports no sap. The life line is gone, and so there is no fruit.

Ordinarily dead wood may still be useful. It may be sawed into lumber, or it may be cut up for firewood to warm the home. In the household of the Lord, however, dead wood is of no use whatever. To emphasize this point the sacred writer speaks of the dead branch of a vine. Even when alive it was useful only inasmuch as it bore fruit, and, apart from the vine, it could not do that much. Of what good is it when dead?

In Biblical times it was common practice to fashion pegs from the branches of sturdy trees. These were driven into the walls of houses for the hanging of pots and vessels and articles of clothing. But no dead branch of a vine could serve such a purpose. It was no good. It lacked strength for a peg on which to hang a hat. It was good for nothing. Dead wood in the Church is like the dead branch of a vine — good for nothing.

The dead wood in the church consists of those who bring forth no fruit. Such are always found in the Church. Three thousand years have passed since the prophet uttered his complaint. There was dead wood then; there is dead wood now.

Every congregation has its dead wood. But the ministry also has its dead wood. In the thirteenth chapter, God said to Ezekiel, "Son of man, prophesy against the prophets of Israel that prophesy, and say thou unto them that prophesy out of their own hearts, Hear ye the word of the LORD." There follows a scathing denunciation of the prophets who do not preach the Word of God. "Thus saith the Lord GOD; Because ye have spoken vanity...." Ignoring the Word of God, they were preaching their own thoughts.

Ezekiel lived in the day of the Babylonian captivity. One of his contemporaries, Ezra, gives us a clear picture of conditions in Israel at the time. What Luther was in modern times, Ezra was in the Old Testament. The Word of God had fallen into neglect, and had been relegated to a secondary position; it was held of less importance than human traditions and doctrines.

As in Luther's day, so in Ezra's day — the Bible existed. We know that Daniel had a Bible in Babylon. However, in the existing Bibles one book was missing entirely, and other books were full of inaccuracies and mistakes, which were either inadvertently made by men who copied Bibles, or were arbitrarily inserted. There were additions and deletions. Ezra's first great task was to collect together and set forth a correct edition of Holy Scripture, an undertaking comparable in magnitude to Luther's translation of the Bible. In this he was assisted by the great Sanhedrin, consisting of 120 members, including Daniel, and his friends, Shadrach, Meshach, and Abed-nego.

Ezra's second task was to restore the true worship of God. He examined practices and usages of the church as they were remembered by old people, who had taken part in them during their youth, or who had learned of them through their parents. Ezra worked for the restoration of the Bible and for true worship with such zeal and success that he won the acclaim of the Jews, who said, "If Moses had not given the law, Ezra would have been worthy of giving it." Later Jews said that Ezra was Malachi, meaning, "Angel of the Lord," be cause he was sent as a messenger of God. Under Ezra the Old Testament Church experienced a reformation like that of the New Testament Church under Luther.

Sad to say, wholesomeness and purity were short-lived. Soon there was again much dead wood. Again the Word of God was neglected, while human traditions and doctrines were preached. Corrupt prophets proclaimed that, through Moses, God published not only the written law, but also an oral law, kept alive from generation to generation by tradition of the elders. The Jews even listed a long line of men through whom, down through the centuries, the oral law was delivered. They dated the list back to the days of Moses. It was all pure fiction, spun out of the fertile imagination of the Talmudists, without any foundation in the Word of God, or in any authentic history. The papists have a similar fictitious line of popes running back through the early centuries, all the way to Peter, whom they have called the first pope.

The written law of Moses and their own oral law were held to be of equal importance and authority. In fact, not the written law but the oral law was the final authority; for the written law, they said, "is in many places obscure, and scanty, and defective, and must, therefore, be interpreted in the light of the oral law." Christ later accused them of having made the Word of God of none effect through their traditions.

These oral laws multiplied and multiplied until a rabbi named Judah collected them in six books. This is the Mishnah, the holy book of the Jews, accepted by them with high veneration, together with the claim that everything contained in it was revealed by God. The comments on it, written by Jewish theologians, make up the two Talmuds, the Babylonian and Judean. Once again there was so much dead wood that only here and there a green branch was still bearing fruit. Such were conditions when the Saviour came. There was a Zacharias, a Simeon, a John the Baptist, but they and a few others made up a small remnant in Israel. The great, great majority was steeped in human traditions and doctrines.

In our Lord's day there was a great show of pseudo-sanctity in the church. Pharisees and priests mumbled prayers in public places. A high priest strutted before the people in royal robes, claiming to be the mouthpiece of God. Before him knelt priests and chief priests, kissing his hand in a show of obedience and veneration. There were great throngs in the crowded courtyards in front of the temple. But the entire religious structure was dead wood. The people sacrificed doves, lambs, and sheep, which were raised on the farms of Caiaphas and Annas. They were sold by spiritual hucksters in the temple, and these again paid high rentals for their concessions to Caiaphas and his associates. John the Baptist, utterly disgusted with all the dead wood, said, "The axe is already laid at the root of the tree." And when the Romans came, chopped it down, and held a match to it, the entire dead and rotten rubbish turned to ashes.

For a time after the day of Christ and the Apostles, the Church flourished as a green tree. But not for long. With the conversion of the Emperor Constantine the bloody centuries of persecution ended, but so did the most glorious missionary era of the Christian Church. Soon the Word of God was again neglected and shrouded with the same old warp and woof of human traditions and doctrines. Again we see the same old display of pomp and show and power. We see the same corruption of God's Word, the same claim for authority equal to that of God's Word, the same commercializing of sacred things. The only new thing that has been added is "Bingo." "Behold, I am against you, saith the Lord GOD."

Humbly, but with grateful hearts, we claim for our Lutheran Church that it is the Gospel Church. Sadly we admit that there is much dead wood. We know what resulted in Germany when rationalism and modernism raised their ugly heads, and when the Word of God was interpreted in the light of human reason. As Jerusalem was destroyed under Nebuchadnezzar and again under the Romans, so Germany also was destroyed — and for the same reason. Destruction and ruin inevitably follow when God is compelled to say, "Behold, I am against you."

However, modernism crept into our country also. Here, too, we have Lutheran bodies full of dead wood, because they do not insist that their pastors accept the Bible as the inspired Word of God. The downfall always begins when the Church neglects the Gospel and trusts in campaigns; when purity of architectural design becomes more important than purity of doctrine; when the study of liturgics is stressed above the study of God's Word; when robes and vestments outmode the robe of Christ's righteousness. It is a sure way of blighting green wood.

Dear brother, if I were being installed here today, and if you were preaching the sermon, I would want you to remind me of the dire consequences throughout the centuries when the light of the Gospel was dimmed by the fog of human doctrines and traditions. You can remain a green and fruit-bearing branch of the vine, which is Christ, only if you preach redemption through Jesus Christ. To preach a single sermon, which does not set forth the doctrine of justification by faith in Christ Jesus, is a sin against the vow of installation. It would mean to whittle a peg out of the dead branch of a vine on which no-one could hang his hope of salvation.

When the prophets in the days of Ezekiel did not preach the Word of the Lord, God said, "they preached vanity." All preaching is vanity — utterly in vain, if it does not answer the question — and it must be the right answer — "What must I do to be saved?" In Christ we have the only Saviour, and we can be saved only by personally accepting the sacrifice which He made for the atonement of our sins by the shedding of His blood.

Knowing the story of your life and knowing you, as I do, I am sure that today you are determined, as Paul was in Corinth, "not to preach anything but Christ, and him crucified." But I also know how determined Satan is to have you do otherwise. You will need to pray, and the members of this congregation will need to pray, that you may remain a green, fruit-bearing branch of the Vine.

I pray, and your brethren here pray, that God may bless you from on high, and make you a blessing to many, so that the Lord's vineyard here may grow and bring forth much fruit. *Amen.*

# 38

## The Preaching of the Gospel Breathes
## Life Into the Dead

### (Installation)
### Ezekiel 37:1-14

*The hand of the* LORD *was upon me, and carried me out in the spirit of the* LORD, *and set me down in the midst of the valley which was full of bones. And caused me to pass by them round about: and behold, there were very many in the open valley; and, lo, they were very dry. And he said unto me, Son of man, can these bones live? And I answered, O Lord* GOD, *thou knowest. Again he said unto me, Prophesy upon these bones, and say unto them, O ye dry bones, hear the word of the* LORD. *Thus saith the Lord* GOD *unto these bones; Behold, I will cause breath to enter into you, and ye shall live: And I will lay sinews upon you, and will bring up flesh upon you, and cover you with skin, and put breath in you, and ye shall live; and ye shall know that I am the* LORD. *So I prophesied as I was commanded: and as I prophesied, there was a noise, and behold a shaking, and the bones came together, bone to his bone. And when I beheld, lo, the sinews and the flesh came up upon them, and the skin covered them above: but there was no breath in them. Then said he unto me, Prophesy unto the wind, prophesy, son of man, and say to the wind, Thus the Lord God; Come from the four winds, O breath, and breathe upon these slain, that they may live. So I prophesied as he commanded me, and the breath came into them, and they lived, and stood up upon their feet, an exceeding great army. Then he said unto me, Son of man, these bones are the whole house of Israel: behold, they say, Our bones are dried, and our hope is lost: we are cut off for our parts. Therefore prophesy and say unto them, Thus saith the Lord God; Behold, O my people, I will open your graves, and cause you to come up out of your graves, and bring you into the land of Israel. And ye shall know that I am the Lord, when I have opened your graves, O my people, and brought you up out of your graves, And shall put my spirit in you, and ye shall live, and I shall place you in your own land: then shall ye know that I the Lord have spoken it and performed it, saith the Lord.*

Years ago, my wife and I visited some of the great churches and cathedrals in Mexico City and its surroundings. In one (if my memory serves me right it was Tepoztlan) we entered a large room, directly behind the altar. A number of trap doors in the floor opened the way to an extensive subterranean vault under the altar. Tier upon tier were niches containing caskets with the remains of the dead. The superstitious people believed they would have an advantage above others if on judgment day their bones were found under an altar. At any rate, there they remained as long as rent was paid for the space. If no one paid the rent, the bones were removed, and cast upon a heap in one corner. Our guide informed us that beneath the spot where we were standing we would find a high stack of human bones. He invited us to descend and see for ourselves. We declined. It was only natural that we asked ourselves, "What will happen down there on the day of resurrection?" Our text tells us what will happen.

In the days of the Babylonian captivity, God took Ezekiel aside and, in a vision, showed him a valley covered with human bones. Ezekiel said, "They were very dry." In this vision God granted the prophet a preview of two coming events; namely, of the restoration of the Kingdom of Israel after the captivity, and of the resurrection of the dead at the end of time.

God commanded Ezekiel to walk all around the valley, so that its awful silence might impress him with the deadness of the dead. And then came the Lord's pointed question, "Son of man, can these bones live?" That has been mankind's most troublesome question ever since the day when death entered the world.

Evidently, the prophet considered it presumptuous to give a direct answer. To him, at that moment, the dead bones spoke only of the permanency of death. Whether all men are created equal may be debatable, but their equality in death was all too apparent at the moment. Death, as the great equalizer, made them all alike, mere relics of something that had been. Shaken out of his reverie by the question, "Son of man, can these bones live?" Ezekiel could only humbly answer, "O Lord GOD, thou knowest."

Then came the word of divine power and authority, "Prophesy upon these bones, and say unto them, O ye dry bones, hear the word of the Lord. Thus saith the Lord GOD unto these bones; Behold, I will cause breath to enter into you, and ye shall live." The prophet spoke as God commanded him to speak. At once, the prophet experienced what we will experience on the last day; the air was filled with the sound of rattling bones, as they came together, "bone to his bone." "Sinews and flesh came up upon them, and the skin covered them above.... But there was no breath in them." The entire valley was covered with bodies, lying there like the body of Adam on the day of his creation, before God breathed into his nostrils.

Again came the voice of the Lord, "Prophesy unto the wind, prophesy, son of man, and say to the wind, Thus saith the Lord GOD; Come from the four winds, O breath, and breathe upon these slain, that they may live." When the prophet spoke as God had authorized him to speak, "the breath came into them." The souls, so long absent from the bodies, returned, "and they stood up upon their feet, an exceeding great army."

Today, my dear young brother, God is ordaining you to prophesy to men that they shall live again. And in your prophecies you are to say, "Thus saith the Lord GOD." You may point out to men how many things indicate the resurrection of the dead — things like man's instinctive conviction that he will live again, or like the seed which falls into the ground, decays, and then springs up again. But your emphasis must always be placed upon the "Thus saith the Lord GOD."

Years ago, in a laboratory, one of my teachers took a penny and dropped it into a solvent. Before our eyes we saw the penny disintegrate and dissolve, until no trace of it remained. Then he added another solution, and the copper reformed itself. "Now," he said, "if we send the copper to the mint to be stamped once more with the proper die, it will again be a penny." Then he added, "Thus God will do on the day of resurrection. He will reassemble our bodies and impress them with His own image. This He will do because He said so." Because God said so, you can confidently say, "I believe in the resurrection of the dead."

Christ, our Lord, said, "The hour is coming when they that are in their graves shall hear his voice, and come forth." He said, "I am the resurrection and the life, he that believeth in me, though he were dead, yet shall he live, and he that liveth and believeth in me shall never die." He could speak with authority, because He Himself arose from the dead, "and became the firstfruits of them that slept."

The theme of Paul's first sermon on a mission field was, "The resurrection of Christ." In his Epistle to the Corinthians he reminded them of the beginning of his work among them. "For I delivered unto you first of all that which I also received, how that Christ died for our sins, according to the scriptures; and that he was buried, and that he rose again the third day according to the scriptures." Emphatically he added, "So we preach, and so ye believed."

In their very first public appearance after Pentecost, Peter and John brought persecution upon themselves because they "preached through Jesus the resurrection from the dead." The philosophers of Athens sneered at Paul, because "he preached

unto them Jesus, and the resurrection." This is the theme
which runs through the Book of Acts and through the Epistles,
"Jesus, and the resurrection of the dead."

How could it be otherwise? The resurrection from the dead
is the aim of all our faith and hope. "Jesus and the Resurrection," this theme should not be reserved for Easter and for
funerals, but should run through all your sermons, Sunday
after Sunday, and year after year. "Jesus and the Resurrection," the two may never be separated. To preach the resurrection of the dead without preaching Jesus is as aimless as
the quarrel between Pharisees and Sadducees concerning the
resurrection. Without Jesus, the thought of a resurrection can
only be terrifying.

Ezekiel's vision of the valley of dry bones also serves as a
picture of man's spiritual condition after the fall into sin. "By
one man sin entered into the world, and death by sin; and so
death passed upon all men, for that all have sinned." As the
ugly figure of sin stalked into paradise, the grim figure of
death came right after it. The twins, temporal death and
eternal death, only God can separate. Always eternal death
is the forerunner of temporal death. Abel died physically because Cain was dead spiritually, but in another sense Adam
killed both. The poison of sin, which infiltrated man's entire
being, affected him spiritually as much as physically. Man
was spiritually blind. His gropings always led him against a
blank wall. He could not find a way back to God and to
eternal life. The Shah Jahan built the Taj Mahal, hoping
that its beauty might hide the ugliness of death; the Pharaohs
constructed the pyramids to preserve their bodies against the
day when, after countless migrations, the souls might return;
Ponce de Leon, searching for the fountain of youth, and
thousands of others, sought to devise means to escape death's
ugly consequences. These all merely revealed how dead they
were spiritually. Sin made of all the earth one vast valley of
dry bones of the dead.

One only could help; and He did. God said to His Son,
"Go, and put a stop to the dying of the creature, which I
created with my own hands, and in my own image; go, and become one like unto them; go, and separate temporal death

from eternal death; go, and convert temporal death into a sweet slumber by saving them from eternal death." When Christ's atoning sacrifice completely satisfied the demands of the Father's justice; when He had perfectly fulfilled the law for us by His holy life; when He had borne the punishment of our sins in His own body on the accursed tree; when the Father raised Him from the dead, and thereby declared all men justified — then once again was heard the rattle of bones, as they joined together, "bone to his bone." Once again the bones of dead men were covered with sinews and flesh, and overlaid with skin. Once again the winds were commanded to breathe life into them. "Many of the dead arose." It was a glorious preview of what will take place on the day of resurrection, when on continents, and islands, and even on the bottom of the sea there will be a mighty rattling of bones, when "all the dead will hear his voice, and come forth."

For forty days after His resurrrection our Lord remained on earth to show Himself alive. Then, on the glorious morning of His ascension, came the highest dignity, honor, and trust, ever conferred upon mortal men. Then He said to His disciples, "As the Father sent me so I send you. Go into all the world and preach the Gospel unto every creature." What He once said to Ezekiel, He now said to all His servants, "Son of man, prophesy that these bones may live."

In the Gospel and in the Sacraments, dear brother, your Saviour provided you with a power over death against which Satan with all his hellish might is helpless. Here you have not only the power to strengthen those who already have been raised from spiritual death, but the enabling force to breathe life into such as are still spiritually dead.

Today you are given the marvelous privilege to preach Jesus and the resurrection in these, your new environments. And with the privilege goes the duty to do so. Today I could speak to you of the many duties of your ministry. But, if you are today determined to do this one thing, to preach Jesus and the resurrection, Sunday after Sunday, and year after year, then all else will follow; for the love of Christ will constrain you. May the Holy Spirit give you grace to say, "This I preach; for this I believe." *Amen.*

# 39

## *Farewell*
### Philippians 1:6

*Being confident of this very thing, that he which hath be-
gun a good work in you will perform it until the day of
Jesus Christ:*

Thirty-nine years ago this week, I came to Baltimore and
Martini. Entering this house of God for the first time, I
was greeted by the members, one of whom said, "Our last pastor served us for eighteen years, and we hope you will remain
with us at least as long." My answer was, "Few pastors remain
eighteen years in one parish." Yet, next Sunday, on the eighty-
ninth anniversary of Martini, exactly thirty-nine years will
have passed since the day I considered eighteen years too long
a span to look ahead. And now, as I look back, I can truly
say, "I have no regrets."

No pastor can close a ministry of forty-six years without a
heart crowded with emotions. For me the day is brightened by
the thought that I will still be a member of the Martini which
I love so deeply, and that I am not losing the friend-
ships of many years.

I said, "I have no regrets." Please do not think me guilty
of a complacent and conceited satisfaction with my work and

conduct. At his very best, any pastor must be adjudged far from perfect. The Saviour says, "When ye have done all these things, say, we have been unprofitable servants." Nor do I say, "I have no regrets," because my ministry here has been so pleasant, sweetened by your love. For this I am, indeed, deeply grateful. Always my wife and I will remember your sympathetic kindness and help in the days and weeks when heavy clouds of sorrow and anxiety hung over the parsonage. Nevertheless, when I say, "I have no regrets," I am thinking of something else.

I was called here to preach the Gospel to you, and to teach you and your children the way to salvation. To this I pledged myself in my installation vow. In all modesty I dare to say, I did that for which I was called. Of this I am certain because I preached the word of God, and not my own. In His word alone there is certainty.

It was near the close of his life when Paul wrote to the Philippians, "Being confident of this very thing, that he which hath begun a good work in you, will perform it until the day of Jesus Christ." "I am confident," Paul says, "I am certain, I am sure." Psychologists tell us that at whatever point we are most insecure we make the loudest and strongest claims to assure ourselves that we really do believe what we say. Hence, preachers will pound their pulpits hardest when they are least sure of what they are saying. But Paul's emphatic assertion did not stem from uncertainty. He said, "It is right for me to think this." The basis for his argument rested on the fact that he had preached to the Philippians what God had revealed to him.

Today I also am confident "that he which hath begun a good work in you, will perform it until the day of Jesus Christ." And my confidence also rests on my certainty that I preached the word of God. A man, whom many of you knew, on his deathbed, said to me, "I have heard you preach for more than twenty-five years, and always it was the same thing: justification by grace through faith in Christ Jesus. You dressed it up differently Sunday after Sunday, but it was always the same thing." Then he added, "I believe that with all my heart, and I want to die in that faith." Nothing in my ministry ever made me happier than to have the man tell me that on his deathbed. "It was always the same thing." Paul also always preached the same thing. He summed up all his preaching when he said, "We preach Christ and him crucified." It was what Christ instructed Paul to preach, and on the day of my installation you exacted from me the promise to preach that to the exclusion of all else. Today, as I return to you the sacred charge you committed to me thirty-nine years ago, I do so with the humble assurance, "Mission accomplished."

In all earthly affairs life is a matter of steering, of always adjusting ourselves to the present, of accommodating ourselves to the changes all around us. Just as the magnetic torpedo, when it leaves the submarine, adjusts its course to any change of direction by the ship, which seeks escape, so must we in ordinary life adjust our course in pursuit of new goals. No one can set the rudder for once and always on the trip over the sea of life.

However, there can be no adjustments in preaching and teaching the way to salvation. There is only one way, and that one way is Christ. He said, "I am the Way." Christ never changes. He is "the same yesterday, and today, and forever." Since He, the Saviour, does not change, there can be no change in the way of salvation.

Many have no security because their faith is based on mere human authority. They naively accept the *Koran,* or the *Book of Mormon,* or the *Science and Health* of Christian Science, though behind these are only the bones and ashes of Mohammed, of Joseph Smith, and of Mary Baker Eddy. Behind the Bible is the living Christ, who said, "Heaven and earth shall pass away, but my word shall not pass away."

Many, many pulpits are occupied by the prophets of uncertainty. They speak of the creation with uncertainty. No one, they argue, can be sure how the world was created — what part God had in it, nor what resulted from chance and accident. No one, they say, can be sure of Christ's origin, nor of His divinity, nor of His resurrection. No one can be sure, they say, that we will arise from the dead, nor can anyone prove the existence of a heaven. However, they preach their uncertainties with a pounding on their pulpits, with a show of erudition, with a showmanship, which despite its buffoonery, attracts a following and wins for them publicity and worldly honor. They preach uncertainty because they are uncertain, and not sure of anything. They destroy the faith of others because they, themselves, have no faith. Their acclaim is short-lived. They disparage Paul's preaching, and speak of Pauline doctrine as something apart from the teaching of Christ. However, long after they are utterly forgotten, Paul will still lead men to Christ because he was not an apostle of uncertainty, but of certainty. He could say, and did say, "I know," "I am persuaded," "I am confident." He could be sure because he preached Christ, whose word is abiding.

Without Christ nothing is sure; everything is uncertain, and we are a mystery to ourselves. Do we possess a soul? What is the soul? What is its destiny? It is all a mystery. You have heard the story of the man who was found hanged in a room whose doors and windows were all locked from the inside. So it could not be murder. How could it be suicide? The rope was tied to a rafter too high for him to have reached, and there was no chair or article of furniture on which he could have stood. The newspapers spoke of a mystery beyond solution. Then an observing person noticed dampness on the floor and ended the mystery. The man had stood on a large cake of ice, which had melted away before he was found hanging. Deep mysteries simply melt away when we know Christ, when we know Him as the Son of God and Saviour of the world. There the mystery ends. We know whence we came and whither we go.

Paul's certainty left him without regret. In the end there was prison and death, but he was not cheerless or despondent. On the contrary, more than ever he was certain, and said, "For me to live is Christ, for me to die is gain." He knew Christ; he had preached Christ; he was saved by Christ and had led others to salvation by introducing them to Christ. Therefore he had no regrets.

It is only because I preached Christ and Him crucified that I have no regrets today. Nothing will be changed here. You will hear a different voice, but you will hear the same message, the same Gospel of salvation. Being certain of this, I have no fears for the future of Martini. Thirty-nine years ago I was told that the blighted area surrounding this church doomed me to become the captain of a sinking ship. But, thanks be to God, the ship did not sink; in fact, it is more seaworthy and sturdy now than it was then. I am confident, as long as the Gospel of Christ is preached here, there will be a future, and I am confident that better days are ahead.

And now, in conclusion, let me say a few words to you, not as a congregation, but as individuals. There is scarcely one here this morning whom I do not call by the first name. We have been too intimate for anything else. I baptized, confirmed, and married many of you. There are few here with whom I have not sorrowed on sad occasions and rejoiced on glad occasions. I am sure, in this respect, there will be no change in the future. But one thing will be changed. I will no longer be your pastor. I hope no one will embarrass me by asking me to do anything which will now be the prerogative and duty of your new pastor. If you would please me, show him the respect, the kindness, and the love which you have shown me. I think you will understand when I say, nothing could hurt me more than if I and the members of my family would be compelled to transfer our membership to another congregation, which we would have to do if my presence should prove to be an embarrassment to my successor. Let us remain friends, but remember that I am no longer your pastor.

May the God of all grace, who permitted us together to grow in Christian fellowship and in the knowledge of salvation, keep us in faith, and continue to bless our beloved Martini, and bring us all, at last, into the presence of our Lord and Saviour, Jesus Christ, to whom be glory forever. *Amen.*